Mary D. Sheldon

Studies in general History

Mary D. Sheldon
Studies in general History
ISBN/EAN: 9783337165932

Printed in Europe, USA, Canada, Australia, Japan
Cover: Foto ©ninafisch / pixelio.de

More available books at **www.hansebooks.com**

STUDIES
IN
GENERAL HISTORY.

BY

MARY D. SHELDON,

FORMERLY PROFESSOR OF HISTORY IN WELLESLEY COLLEGE,
AND TEACHER OF HISTORY IN OSWEGO
NORMAL SCHOOL, N.Y.

Teacher's Manual.

"*It is impossible that the history of any state should possess any interest unless it show some sort of development.*" — J. R. SEELEY.

BOSTON:
D. C. HEATH & COMPANY.
1894.

TO

My best of Masters,

Professor J. R. Seeley,

This book is most gratefully
dedicated.

PREFACE.

THEY say my "Studies" are hard, and I am glad to hear it, for so in truth they should be, since history itself is hard. Our text-books in this subject have been mostly manuals of the results of this study, presented in more or less attractive literary form. They have given no chance for any genuine work; and yet the study of history demands most serious work; like mathematics, it involves logic; like language, it demands analysis and fine discrimination of terms; like science, it calls for exact observation; like law, it needs the cool, well-balanced judgment; beyond all these, it requires the highest, fullest use of the sympathetic imagination. In fact, no study is more difficult; none calls more completely on all the mental powers, none affords the mind more generous play.

It is indeed easy to read and then repeat: "Magna Charta laid the foundation of English liberty"; "The Athenian people were brave, patriotic, magnanimous, and highly-cultured"; "The government of Lewis XIV. was arbitrary, corrupt, unjust, extravagant"; but to read, or even to learn such sentences as these by heart, is not to study, or even to touch the study of history; these are mere statements of the results of historical research; before he can name his work "study," the pupil must have found out some results for himself, by exercising his own powers upon the necessary "raw material" of history; let him read Magna Charta; let him see the Athenian people in action in their contemporary world; let him have the facts of French organization and administration under Lewis XIV.; let him look, and look again, like Agassiz' famous pupil at the fish, until he sees the essential spirit, purpose, or character displayed within these words and deeds and figures; thus he becomes a genuine student. By such practice, he learns, as a practical historian, to interpret social and political forms and facts, as the biologist learns to interpret living organisms by the actual dissection of a few typical forms, or as the mathematician fits himself to wrestle with new complications by conquering well-set, formal problems; in each case, actual work is done; and nought but actual work knits us to reality.

In teaching history in higher grades, three points must always be in mind: first, to give each student independent work; next, to subject the results of solitary, individual thought to the freest criticism and discussion in the class-room; last of all, the accepted results of the collective labor must be arranged in compact and logical order, and stowed away in memory. By the solitary study of the individual, the mind gains power and originality; by the "free lance in a free field" of class-room work, the mind gains courage, sharpness, speed, and generous temper; by the strict, close sifting of study and discussion, it gains concentration, clearness, and breadth.

This mode of instruction is, in its essence, the famous "Seminary" method, first employed in Germany, and of late introduced into our own leading colleges. To render its advantages available for large classes with limited libraries, and a limited course of historical study, I have made these two books: the Student's edition contains the material and the problems for independent study; the Teacher's Manual contains the answers to these problems, embodied in tabulations, and a running commentary of text, which may serve as suggestive for the discussions and the summaries demanded by the class-room.

As for the advantage of this method to the *teacher*, I can only say that I can but hope it will save him the tedium of the treadmill; that it will bring him day by day the living, sympathetic touch of youthful thought and feeling; and that, in time, the world may read with fairer, clearer meaning to himself.

MARY SHELDON BARNES.

TABLE OF CONTENTS.

	PAGE
PREFACE	v–vi
CIVILIZED WORLD BEFORE 776 B.C.	1–7
Introductory	1–3
A. Study on Egypt	3–4
B. Study on Tigro-Euphrates Valley	5
C. Study on Phœnicia	6
D. Study on Judæa	7
HELLAS	8–35
A. Study on Heroic Age	9–13
B. Study on Historic Greece	13–21
C. Study on the Persian Wars	21–27
D. Study on the Athenian Leadership; Age of Perikles	27–33
E, F. Study on Period 431–338	33–35
THE HELLENISTIC, OR ALEXANDRIAN CONQUESTS AND KINGDOMS	36–39
ROME	39–83
Introductory	39–40
A, B. I. Study on Regal Rome and Præ-Punic Republic	41–46
B. II. Study on Republican Rome, Punic Period	46–52
B. III. Study on Republican Rome, Post-Punic Period	53–58
C. I. Study on Pagan Empire, Augustus to Diocletian	58–65
Teutonic Barbarians before 476 A.D.	65–68
C. II. Christian Empire, Constantine to Charlemagne	68–83
A. Christian Empire under Roman Control	69–75
B. and C. The West under Barbarian Control; Empire of Charlemagne	76–83

TABLE OF CONTENTS.

	PAGE
EUROPEAN HISTORY, 814–1880	84–167
Introductory	84–85
A. Early Mediæval Period; Charlemagne to the Crusades, 814–1095	86–94
B. Study on Crusading Period	94–100
C. Study on Later Mediæval Period	100–114
D. Renaissance and Reformation Era	115–127
E. Modern Europe	128–167
I. The "Old Régime," 1648–1789	128–140
Aa. In Europe in General	128–134
Ab. In France	134–140
II. French Revolution and Wars of Napoleon	141–149
French Revolution	141–144
Napoleonic Rule	145–146
Prussian Revolution	146–149
III. The Nineteenth Century	150–167
In General	150–162
Special Study on Germany	162
Special Study on Italy	162–166
Socialism	166

STUDIES IN GENERAL HISTORY.

Teacher's Manual.

STUDIES IN GENERAL HISTORY.

[N.B. — All page references are to the Students' Edition.]

THE CIVILIZED WORLD BEFORE 776 B.C.

BEFORE the "Studies" are begun at all, the teacher should have a preliminary discussion of the meaning of the word "civilization." I have found it a very good plan to give the students for the first day's lesson this requirement for home work, — "Make a list of all the reasons you have for calling yourselves civilized." You will find when the answers are brought the next day that you have plenty of material for discussion and analysis. Since the greatest masters hesitate to *define* the word civilization, it will probably be best in the class-room work simply to aim at some general, but clear ideas, which may strengthen and elucidate its meaning. The material brought by the pupils in answer to your question will probably enable you to make some such analysis as follows : —

CIVILIZATION.

Proofs of.
    Houses, clothing, furniture, etc.
    Railroads, roads, telegraphs, post-offices, etc.
    Books, pictures, schools, etc.
    Churches, societies, etc.
    The family and the home, etc.
    Government, courts of law, etc.

Directions of.
    Material, industrial, and commercial.
    Intellectual and æsthetic.
    Religious.
    Social.
    Political.

Present Area of European (progressive) Civilization.

In discussing the present area of European (or Aryan) civilization, the teacher may ask the pupils how this civilization is different from that of China and India, and note that European civilization is marked by *progress* as opposed to immobility. With some classes of pupils it may not be amiss to ask what classes of people in Europe and America are most civilized, requiring some proof for the answer given, and calling attention to the fact that in the most civilized countries, civilization in its higher directions is most widely *diffused* among all classes, although even in these countries, it is far from being equally so.

This whole discussion should be treated simply and largely, giving room and freedom for all opinions, without any anxiety for particularly close or definite results, which are indeed undesirable in dealing with such a subject.

The pupils are now ready for the questions on p. 3. They will note that Egypt, the Tigro-Euphrates valley, Phœnicia, and Judæa, were each so protected from easy invasion, by mountains, rivers, deserts, and seas, and at the same time so fortunate in climate and so easily supported by agriculture or commerce, that men in these countries could devote a part, at least, of their time and strength to the various arts of civilization. This Oriental civilization would first enter Europe in the South, both because here Europe is easily reached from the East, and fairly protected from invasion, being peninsular southward and guarded by mountain-barriers northward.

If there be time, it will be interesting just here to notice the various modern states of Europe and see how far their political boundaries have natural defenses, Prussia being a very good example of a state without, and England of a state with, natural boundaries. If the pupils have difficulty in seeing that civilization will grow fastest where the protection from invasion is greatest, other things being equal, simply ask them to name some of the things which civilized people make and do, and they will soon see that time and quiet, and therefore a certain amount of peace, are necessary to civilization. This point being made, they are ready to see how the deserts and mountains, rivers and seas, were so placed as to allow an early civilization along the Nile and Euphrates valleys, while their fertile soil, capable of feeding thousands with little toil, gave whole classes leisure for varied industries. It has been suggested to me, moreover, that the rivers that traverse these great valleys made an easy means of communication between the various parts of their respective lands, — a point of great importance.

}.

A. STUDY ON EGYPT.

The answers given to the questions on pp. 7 and 15, and on p. 3 concerning Egypt, may be summarized as follows : —

EGYPT, 4000 (?) – 1250 (?) B.C.

Natural Advantages for Early Civilization.
    Protection from invasion by
        desert.
        seas.
    Abundance of food easily procured, by reason of
        climate.
        fertile soil.
        level surface.
        annual inundation of the Nile.
    Easy internal communication by means of the Nile.

Organization of Society (Oriental): aristocratic, theocratic, and monarchic, centred at Memphis and Thebes : —
    King : ruler, general, builder,
    Priests : scholars, authors, and officials, } land-owners.
    Nobles : soldiers and officials,
    Common people : traders and artizans : embalmers, stone-cutters, engravers, jewellers, scribes, carpenters, cabinet-makers weavers, potters, glass-makers, etc., etc.
    Serfs, slaves, and captives : worked the land and served in the household, hewed and carried the stone, and made the brick for great public works.

Egypt. — *Continued.*
Characteristics of People and Civilization.
    Political:
        absolutism; centralization of industrial, religious, and political life in the king, supported by land-owning privileged classes.
    Social: inequality.
    Industrial: high material development.
    Moral:
        obedience and kindness most admired.
        standard of morality high.
    Religious:
        polytheistic nature-worship, with monotheistic tendencies.
        absolute trust in immortality.
        belief in the ability of the gods to help men.
        close union of religion with the state, as shown in —
            importance of temples and privileges of priests.
            sacredness of king.
    Intellectual:
        attainment of culture in —
            literature.
            mathematics; geometry.
            astronomy.
            medicine.
        great inequality of culture.
    Æsthetic:
        admiration for solidity and size.
Enduring Remains of Civilization.
    Monuments: pyramids, temples.
    Objects of fine and industrial art: sculpture, jewelry, etc.
    Knowledge: geometrical, mathematical, medical.
    Literature: theology, morals, poetry, fiction, historic records.

In summarizing these results the teacher will find it necessary perhaps to give such terms as Oriental, monarchic, aristocratic, theocratic, absolutism, polytheism, monotheism, but in each case he should first give the pupils themselves the chance to apply the term. And when given, the word should be defined as exactly as possible by the pupils, in order that the teacher may be sure of its being understood in its application.

B. STUDY ON THE TIGRO-EUPHRATES VALLEY.

This study may be summarized as follows: —

TIGRO-EUPHRATES VALLEY.

Natural Advantages for Early Civilization.
    Same as in Egypt, the Tigris and Euphrates taking the place of the Nile.

Organization of Society.
    Similar to that of Egypt (Oriental).

Characteristics of People and Civilization.
    Political and Social:
        as in Egypt, but centred at Babylon and Nineveh.
    Industrial: similar to that of Egypt.
    Moral:
        admiration for power.
        desire of wealth.
    Religious:
        polytheistic belief.
        belief in the power of the gods in human affairs.
        close union of religion with the state.
    Intellectual:
        attainment of culture in
            literature.
            mathematics.
            astronomy.
        inequality of culture.
    Æsthetic: admiration for the rich and brilliant.

Enduring Remains.
    Objects of industrial art.
    Astronomical knowledge.
    Historic records (clay cylinders).
    Reliefs and sculptured figures of deities.[1]

In summarizing *B*, particular attention should be called to the fact that the king is very positively the centre, not only of religious, but of industrial and intellectual life; in fact, the king, his palaces and temples, embody and include the civilization of Babylon and Nineveh.

---

[1] The object of the stone lions and bulls was not so much æsthetic as protective, magic qualities evidently being ascribed to them. (See p. 18.)

C. STUDY ON PHŒNICIA.

In this study the trade and commerce of the Phœnicians must be emphasized, and the pupils will see that ship-building, navigation, and some manufactures are necessary to a people living by trade; that the Phœnicians would find the best markets among civilized peoples, whose wants were greatest, and that by virtue of their occupation they were at once the greatest learners and the greatest teachers of antiquity: on the one hand, observing the geography, the manners and customs, the arts and industries of all the people among whom they traded; on the other, diffusing this knowledge by interchanging from land to land the various products of the Mediterranean basin. There is much proof that through their agency civilization began to urge its way into Europe along the line of the Greek coasts and islands. Summarize as follows: —

PHŒNICIA.

Natural Advantages of Position.
   Protected from invasion by mountains and the sea.
   On the road from Egypt to Mesopotamia.

Character of People and Culture.
   Industrial and commercial, centring in coast cities of Phœnicia, and in trading-posts (colonies).
   Great variety of occupations, as in Egypt and Mesopotamia, adding navigation, ship-building, lumbering, and mining; slave-dealing, dyeing, ivory-carving.

Enduring Remains of Civilization.
   Objects of industrial art throughout Mediterranean region (glass, pottery, metal-work).
   Knowledge of navigation, its methods, and routes.[1]
   The leading *Alphabets*.

In discussing the general questions on p. 25, let the interpretation of answers be very generous, simply maintaining this point: that the Oriental civilizations were prominently material, with germs of higher types appearing in their midst.

---

[1] The finding of tin for bronze was, according to Lenormant and Chevallier, one of the chief aims of Phœnician commerce.

D. STUDY ON JUDÆA.

In this study the teacher will of course be careful to work entirely from the historical standpoint, avoiding any possible theological or sectarian discussion. I have taken special pains to present Judæa just as I have presented Egypt or Phœnicia, in order that the student may see its historical *relations*.

The following summary may be useful as a guide: —

JUDÆA.

Advantages of Position.
    Protected from invasion by mountains, deserts, and the sea.
    Vicinity to Phœnicia and Egypt.

Organization of Society: theocratic, monarchic.

Characteristics of People and Culture.
    Political:
        close union of church and state.
        predominance of priestly and prophetic influence.
    Religious:
        monotheism, mixed with polytheism.
        close relation of religion and practical life.
    Moral:
        high moral standard imposed by faith.
        great admiration for mercy and justice.

Enduring Remains of Civilization.
    The monotheistic faith.
    Books of the Old Testament.

With the material easily accessible in the Old Testament, the teacher may, if he thinks it desirable, carry this study still further, and note that the Jews were eminently a race of shepherds, farmers, warriors, and priests, with a serious, poetic temperament easily seen in all their literature.

In discussing the answers to the questions on p. 29, the teacher should allow the utmost freedom of opinion, simply requiring that any position taken should be sustained by facts. It is well to allow the pupils to feel that oftentimes there is a reasonable difference of opinion, while at the same time he should be led to understand that only those opinions are respectable which have some sound basis in reality. Thus, while there can hardly be a question but that among the Jews, the pure and upright priest, or the righteous valiant king were the popular ideals, and that among the Assyrians wealth was regarded above all things, it may very justly be questioned whether piety or power was the ruling ideal among the Egyptians; probably both ideals should be admitted.

The following questions and topics are given as suggestions for essays or for dictation for examination: —

What can a watch teach us of its makers? What characteristics of Egyptian art still strike us as admirable? Aside from religion, name two or three points in which our civilization is superior to that of the Egyptians. What can the Temple of Solomon teach us historically? The greatness of Rameses. The palace of Sargon. The Phoenician sailor. The captive Jew in Babylon. Our Oriental debt.

HELLAS.

STUDY ON MAP OF GREECE.

After the preliminary study of the map of Europe, the pupils will easily answer the questions on the geography of Greece, and will see that while agriculture and grazing may be found throughout the country, Laconia is especially fitted for agriculture, Arcadia for grazing, while Attica, adapted to fishing and mining, most naturally invites, by its position, the trade of Asia and the islands. As for the actual relations of Greece and the civilization of Asia and Egypt, the myths (see pp. 33 and 34) indicate that Greece owed her start in civilization to the older countries.

From the answers given by the pupils the teacher summarizes somewhat as follows: —

GREECE.

Geographic Advantages.
> Small states with natural defences.
> Eastward opening harbors.

Vicinity to older civilizations.
Vicinity of eastward leading islands.
Insular and temperate climate.
Variety of products, ∴ [1]
Variety of occupation.
> Agriculture (Laconia).
> Fishing, grazing (Arcadia).
> Quarrying, mining, trade (Attica).

A. STUDY ON HEROIC AGE; HOMERIC GREECE.

The teacher should not undertake to summarize any of the work in *A* until the studies on pp. 37, 39, 42, and 46 have been thoroughly mastered and discussed; he may then tabulate as follows: —

A. HOMERIC GREECE.

Peculiar Institutions.
> Amphictyony:
>> Bound together by kinship and faith.
>
> Amphictyonic Council:
>> Religious league, with Delphic Oracle as its centre.

Political Organization (Monarchic).
> King:
>> Leads in council.
>> Leads in war.
>> Law-giver and priest.
>> Supported by
>>> plunder.
>>> gifts.
>>> produce of his own lands.
>>> sale of war-captives as slaves.
>
> Council of Elders:
>> Advises and persuades
>>> king.
>>> people.
>>
>> Hears proposals.
>> Judges the people.

---

[1] ∴ = *therefore*, wherever used.

Homeric Greece. — *Continued.*
>General Assembly of people (Agora; market-place meeting):
>>Hears announcements of king and princes.
>>Expresses public opinion
>>>by shouting (approval).
>>>by silence (disapproval).

Social Organization: Aristocratic and patriarchal, consisting of
>Classes:
>>Nobles; chiefs.
>>Freemen (common people).
>>Slaves
>>>bought.
>>>stolen.
>>>captured.
>
>Patriarchal,[1] monogamic families.

Characteristics of Civilization.
>Political:
>>Participation of all free men in the government.
>>Value of public opinion.
>
>Social:
>>Patriarchal power tempered toward women by
>>>public opinion.
>>>religion.
>>>affection.
>>
>>Slavery, mild.
>>Amusements, healthful and developing, consisting of
>>>physical contests.
>>>music.
>>>dancing.
>>>story-telling.
>>
>>Habits of equality, simplicity, hospitality.
>
>Industrial and commercial:
>>Sources of material civilization, — Oriental, notably Phœnician and Egyptian.
>>Great variety of occupation and interest (see list of gods, p. 36).
>>Rapid growth of trade between various parts of Greece, encouraged by easy water communication and varied productions.

---

[1] In the case of the absence or death of the father, the son takes his place, as in the case of Telemachus.

Religious:
    Belief, polytheistic and anthropomorphic,—
        Gods thought to be
            immortal.
            of superhuman power.
            subordinate to Zeus.
            influential and interested in human affairs.
            persuaded by
                hymns.
                sacrifices.
                prayers.
                obedience.
        Future life regarded as
            shadow of the present.
            undesirable and gloomy.
    Close relation of religion and life.
Intellectual and æsthetic:
    Cultivation of music and poetry through religion.
    Beginning of sculpture and architecture.

Permanent Remains of Homeric Age.
    Homeric poems: Iliad and Odyssey.
    Fortifications at Mycenæ, in the Troad, and at other prehistoric sites.
    Objects of industrial work (pottery, metal-work) found at above sites.

The teacher may find that the work on the Homeric age occupies what seems a disproportionate part of his time. My own experience has proved to me that *a slow and thorough beginning made here pays*, and that time is actually made by leisurely conscientious work at the opening. In looking over the summary, the teacher must realize that the mind of the pupil for the first time entering history, finds many new and great ideas to assimilate; fundamental ideas, also, several of them associated with new and difficult terms, with which he needs to be familiar through all his work. I cannot sufficiently emphasize this point.

In the Amphictyony, for instance, he meets with a thoroughly characteristic organization of antiquity, namely, a society held together by the bonds of a common faith, and a common kinship, real or assumed. He should be helped to understand it by reference to the Scottish clans, and to the churches and families of his own vicinity. By such reference he may be led to imagine the strength and value of these ancient bonds of union, as giving real fighting power. In the political and social organization he should clearly apprehend in its large and simple features the little aristocratic state, where neither the king nor the slave is far removed from the mass of freemen; by comparing the size of the Greek states with that of Egypt or Assyria, he will readily see that in a small state the king cannot easily remove himself from the very presence of the people and the consequent pressure of their opinions in regard to his actions; while such a small state cannot well enrich itself nor its king by any other means than those of honest labor, since it cannot seize upon the wealth acquired by larger powers. Special pains should be taken that the *Agora*, or General Assembly, is understood as the actual democratic meeting of all adult freemen in the market-place, on any occasion when the presence of the whole people is required, either to give notice of an expedition or a danger or to announce a law; the imagination should be stimulated to conceive clearly of a state of affairs where all common news comes by hearsay, and all common interests must be discussed by word of mouth; in short, of days when there was neither a newspaper, a telegraph, nor a post-office. The importance of the Agora as the safeguard of liberty will then appear double, and it will be clearly perceived that it was the *organ of public opinion*. The point may be illustrated by the meeting of boys in the playground to talk over some common project or expedition.

In discussing amusements, great stress should be laid on their admirable effect in developing physical and artistic excellence.

In studying religious characteristics, note that the gods are like men: (*a*) Physically; they have the parts of the human body, and feel physical needs. (*b*) Emotionally; they hate, fear, love. (*c*) Socially; they also live in the patriarchal style. In other words, the Greek gods are of the complete anthropomorphic type. Although itself below the more spiritual and ideal type of the Hebrew Deity, it may be well to note in passing its superiority to the conceptions of Egypt or Assyria in its influence on human life. So far as possible, the joyous nature of the worship, and its influence on the temper of the people, should be emphasized.

In general, the Greek migrations are southward and eastward; the early movement toward Thessaly is perhaps explained by its comparative size and fertility.

Topics and Questions for Examinations and Essays.—What is the historic value of the Homeric poems? A comparison of Homeric Greece and of the Jews in patriarchal times (Abraham and Ulysses). What was the probable, and what was the certain, influence of the Trojan War on civilization? What traces of nature-worship in the Greek mythology, and what evidences of divine power seen in each of the natural objects thought to be under special divine dominion? A scene at the Lion-gate of Mycenæ, 1000 B.C. Agamemnon's departure from Mycenæ. What points of resemblance between the Greek and Jewish faith? What fundamental difference?

B. STUDY OF HISTORIC GREECE, OR HELLAS, 776–500.

The map, pp. 44, 45, at once reveals that the Greeks were of essentially maritime habit, settling the coasts of every richly productive land within their reach, while their locations at river-mouths and on easily accessible shores show that their colonies were in reality trading-posts. The varied productions of the Greek lands and the varied occupations of the Greek people encouraged the calling of the merchant and sailor, while at the same time it scattered the Greeks here and there along the fertile Mediterranean coasts, preventing any strong political or territorial unity, but making them a strong civilizing force among the barbarous nations.

The whole study on p. 47 should be treated very freely and conversationally, a number of the questions admitting of more than one answer. Here, if he has not done so before, the teacher should impress upon the pupils that, to early traders, the water-ways are by far the easiest, cheapest, and safest roads for travel and commerce.

So far as it is desirable to summarize the answers to these questions, they will be found embodied in the following general tabular view of *B*. 1 : —

GENERAL HELLENIC DEVELOPMENT, 776–490.

Organizations and Institutions of Period.
  Colonies: trading-posts, united to mother-cities by kinship and worship.
  Aristocratic tribal states: examples, Sparta, Attica; bonds of union, common descent (kinship) and worship.
  Olympic games,[1] forming the centre of a loose religious Hellenic union (*cf.* Delphi).

Characteristics of Period.
  Growth of colonies and commerce
    about Black Sea and Bosphorus (*Byzantium*).
    about Ægean.
    in Magna Græcia (*Syracuse*).
  Tendencies to Hellenic union seen in
    religion:
      games, — Olympic, Pythian, Nemean, etc.
      Delphic Oracle.
      amphictyonies.
      sacred war.
    language and literature [2] (Homer).

---

[1] In reckoning Olympiads, it is to be remembered that the first Olympiad does not count for four years; and so, to find the date of the fifteenth Olympiad, one must multiply four by fourteen, instead of by fifteen, and subtract the result from 776 B.C.

[2] If the pupils do not think of this, it may be well to remind them that all outsiders were called by the Greeks "Barbarians," that is, *men who "babble," or speak so that they cannot be understood.* Tell them, too, that Homer was recited and sung in every city and village of Greece.

Tendency to Spartan leadership seen in
    Olympic games.
    Spartan conquests.
    Lydian request for Spartan alliance.
Revolt against oligarchy, ending in "tyranny."
Intellectual, industrial, and artistic impulse
    seen in
        poetry (lyric).
        science (*philosophy*).
        architecture and sculpture.
        working in metal, stone, clay.
    developing along the lines of Greek life and history, ∴
        original and national.
    encouraged by
        religion.
        the "Tyrants."
General diffusion of excellence
    throughout Greek settlements of Asia Minor and the Islands.
    among all free citizens.
Strong influence of religion seen in
    Delphic Oracle.
    games.
    art and literature.
    founding of colonies.
Ideals of the period:
    the gentleman.
    the athlete (victor at Olympia).
    the good and honored citizen.
    the poet, singer, and thinker.
Type of civilization, — commercial, intellectual, artistic.

All these points might also be summarized under the headings, political, social, religious, etc., and it might be well to ask the students so to arrange the various points as an exercise in classification.

In general, it should be strongly impressed upon the mind of the pupil that the bonds of Greek union during this period were worship and kinship; that these bonds not only united them in tribes, classes, cities, and amphictyonies, but that they separated them from *barbarians*, the men of foreign speech and faith; nor is it perhaps unsafe to follow Curtius in assigning great importance to the cohesive force exercised by the Delphic Oracle, which was a centre of knowledge as well as of faith.

But no cohesive force could stand against the strength of local interests. It will be noted through this whole time that each little state, centred in its own little city, acted for itself, fought for itself, and founded its own colonies; Sparta alone sometimes interfered in general Greek affairs, and thus asserted her superior strength.

It will be readily perceived that all the tendencies and organizations of this period followed naturally from those of the Homeric age, with a strengthening of the commercial, religious, and intellectual spirit. The heroes of the Trojan War and the Argonautic Expedition were the precursors of the adventurous traders and colonists; and the men who never fought a battle but with the favor of the gods, the ancestors of those who founded their colonies by the advice of Apollo.

B. II. 1. SPARTA, 776–490 B.C.

Political Organization.
    In form: a limited monarchy.
    In reality: an oligarchic democracy, bound together by religion, kinship, and training.

Social Organization.
    For Spartans: communistic, and entirely subordinate to the state and the army.

Results of the Lycurgan Organization and Institutions.
    Political:
        Spartan leadership in Greece for that period.
    Social:
        Subordination of the individual and the family to the state.
        Importance and influence of women.
        Simplicity, and even rudeness of manners.
    Personal:
        Scorn of any labor other than military.
        High physical development, — strength and beauty.
        Spartan ideal, — the warrior, athlete, and patriot.

In the above study, the phrase, "oligarchic democracy," may seem like a genuine "Irish bull," nor can I say that I at all approve of it, since it is only clear to one who knows what it means. What it does mean is this,— that, while the Spartan body within itself was as pure a working democracy as the world has ever seen, yet, since that body was limited in number, and ruled over a large population of Laconians, who had absolutely no share in the government, it was, as regarded these Laconians, an oligarchy; and throughout the Greek history it will be seen that the Spartan spirit and the Spartan sympathy is aristocratic. Even in this period, we find her always opposed to the man of the people, the "Tyrant."

B. II. 2. ATHENS, 776–490 B.C.

Before Solon, 776-594 B.C.
- Political organization:
  - Aristocracy of clan-elders (Eupatrids), distinguished from other tribesmen by birth and worship.
- Social organization:
  - *Tribal*, the people bound together by kinship and worship into
    - families, forming
    - clans, in turn forming
    - brotherhoods, in turn forming
  - *Four Ionic Tribes*, political units of the City-state.
- [N.B. — Tribesmen alone form the state.]

Changes of Solon, 594 B.C.
- In organization:
  - Aristocracy of birth changed to a timocracy; that is, wealthy as well as high-born tribesmen admitted to power.
  - Community of worship given to all tribesmen.
  - Slavery for tribesmen abolished.
  - Publicity and sacredness of common law.
- In tendency:
  - Development of equality.
  - Limitation of individual by the state.
  - Liberation of individual from family.

ATHENS. — *Continued.*
      Recognition of value of wealth and industry.
      Encouragement of labor and trade.
      Development of unity and freedom by
          loosening of the fixed bonds of birth.
          extension of a common worship.

The Pisistratid Tyranny (*Demagogism*).
    Organized according to forms of Solon's constitution.
    Based on
      local jealousies of Mountain, Plain, and Shore.[1]
      personality of Pisistratus, —
        eloquence.
        geniality.
        tact and intellect.
      ignorance, sympathy, and superstition of the multitude.
      wealth of Pisistratus.
      hired military forces.
    Justified by
      public improvements in
        roads.
        trade.
      patronage of art, science, poetry.
    Caused to fall by
      abuse of the tyrannical power.
      reaction against it.
      ambition of the Alcmæonids.
      opposition of Delphi and Sparta.

Changes of Clisthenes.
    In organization (*Democracy*):
      The kinship bond abolished in politics.[2]
      The tribe of demesmen replaces that of kinsmen in politics.
      The *deme*, or parish, instead of the family, becomes the
        fundamental unit, its men united by a common
        residence and a common worship.
      All free inhabitants become *citizens*.

---

[1] The local jealousies, of course, were strong, because of local interests; to this was added, in the case of the Mountaineers, the desperation of poor men who have nothing to lose.

[2] In social life, of course the kinship bond always remains; and in Greece probably, as well as elsewhere, the "first families" had many things after "their way."

tendency:
>   Development of democracy.
>   Development of unity by
>   > introduction of new worships.
>   > abolition of distinctions of birth between Ionians and Perioeki.

General Character of Athenian History, 776–490 B.C.
>   Constant changes toward equality, democracy, and unity.
>   Parallelism of political, social, and religious distinctions.
>   Widening distribution of political power.
>   Growth of the state in size, numbers, and interests.
>   Gradual liberation of individuals.

In this, the pupil meets with his first serious study of constitutional development, and *the teacher should by no means begrudge the time necessary* to a complete understanding of each stage. The student must have clearly in mind that before the time of Clisthenes the four Ionic tribes form the Athenian state, without reference to the Metics, that the changes of Solon apply simply to Ionic tribesmen, and that in every development of the constitution the place and form of the old Greek bonds of union, kinship and faith, are still respected, though constantly enlarged and loosened, while of these two the common worship is the stronger and gives presumptive evidence of common kin. While these ideas are in reality simple, yet their novelty makes them at first hard to "sense," and time is the one element necessary to their understanding. Thorough work here will save time in all the following constitutional studies.

In Pisistratus, we have a study of that interesting phenomenon, the "man of the people" turned "Tyrant"; the most important point to discuss is the relation between the Tyrant, the ignorant mass, and the constitutional form; and it should be clearly understood that a Tyrant of this type always finds his counterpart in the ignorance or stupidity of his supporters, and that constitutional forms avail little without general intelligence to use them.[1] To come no closer home, it will be well to

---
[1] "I hold all Rome guilty of this Nero." — *Thorndale.*

cite the parallel case of Napoleon III. The full-grown Tyrant, however, is a political teacher, and he never appeared twice in the same Greek state. In Athens, he called out the institution of ostracism, as local party conflicts forced into the constitution the separation of the demes of the same tribe.

In the constitution of Clisthenes we meet with the most radical constitutional change known to antiquity. Before his time, the men born into the same clan belonged together, no matter where they dwelt; unity existed alone in faith and blood-relationship. But he drew neighbors together into the same parish, so that men who *dwelt* together irrespective of blood-relationship should be called by a common name and worship at a common shrine. In other words, he made the land, the common *father-land*, the bond of unity. Though this was his fundamental change, he dared not ignore the old Greek bonds, and so gave to each of his new tribes, mixed of Ionians and Metics, a local hero for common worship, from whom it took its tribal name, as if in direct descent. From this time on, then, we find Ionian and Ionic merged in the larger names of Athenian and Attic.

Before the time of Solon the "Homeric Assembly of Elders" had crowded out of power both the King and the body of freemen; from Solon's time power is turned more and more into the channels of the "agora." But throughout the constitutional development, we never lose sight of the primitive Homeric organization; the magistrates replace the King, the Areopagus and the Senates replace the Assembly of Elders; while the market-place meeting grows into a thoroughly compacted Ecclesia, with large and definite powers.

Suggestions for Essay and Examination Work. — The landing of the Greeks in Illyria. Journal of a Greek sailing from Athens to Phasis. The importance of Byzantium. Which most strongly unites men, religion or commerce, and why? Why is common speech a bond of union? In what ways were the various contemporaneous nations and tribes real barbarians compared with the Greeks, 776–500 B.C.? A day at Olympia. Letter of a Milesian merchant from

Delphi. Was the Greek Tyrant a good or an evil? (Debate.) By what marks would you have known yourself in a Greek state had you been suddenly placed in Athens, 510 B.C., not knowing the language? What geographical fact accounted for the political configuration of Greece and its leading business interest? How far is Sparta a suggestive model? Dialogue between a Spartan and Athenian. The civilizing forces at work, 600 B.C. What would have been the fate of Solon and Clisthenes respectively, had they changed places with each other in time, but not in principles? What lesson can we Americans draw from the story of Pisistratus?

C. STUDY ON PERSIAN WARS, 490–479 B.C.

The study on p. 72 is so exceedingly easy that it may be well simply to make an informal conversation of it, without asking for any home study upon it. Its results, together with those of studies on pp. 76, 80, 82, 85, 87, may be summarized something as follows: —

GENERAL COMPARISON OF ANTAGONISTS.

	Hellenic.	*Persian.*
Territory is	maritime, colonial, scattered, with natural divisions.	agricultural, continental, compact, with arbitrary divisions.
Population is	of one race, speech, and faith.	mixed of many races, tongues, and faiths.
Civilization is	Occidental; that is, diffused.	Oriental; that is, centralized, exclusive.
Governments tend to	democracy and local independence.	despotism, centralization.
Soldiers are	citizens fighting for their own possessions and *independence*.	subjects fighting to gain more *wealth* for their king.

[N.B. — This table can only be started after the study on p. 72; it must be extended and completed by means of the study on p. 76, where additional points are made. At its close, the clear impression should be left on the mind of the pupil that the Persian empire was an enormous heterogeneous compound, massed together by conquerors as a great estate, from which to draw revenues and forces for their private ends; while Greece, or Hellas, was a loose union of citizen-communities, bound together by common sympathies and modes of thought, but full of independent, individual life, each community existing and gathering resources for its own citizens.]

FIRST PERSIAN WAR.

Causes of the War.
  Desire of Darius for wealth of Naxos and Athens.
  Desire of Darius to punish Athens.
  Desire of Hippias for restoration to power.
  Independence of Athens.

Important Events of the War.
  Ionian revolt, and Athenian alliance with it.
  Persian invasion of Greece.
  Battle of *Marathon*, 490 B.C., won by *Miltiades*.
    10,000 Greeks (Athenians) conquer 100,000 Persians.
  Retreat of Persians; end of first war.

Character, Relations, and Tendencies of the Hellenes, as shown in this War.
  General tendency to democratic governments, seen in
    Naxos.
    cities of Asia Minor.
    Athens.
  Democracies opposed by
    aristocracies (Naxos).
    tyrants (Miletus, Athens).
    Darius (Ionian revolt).
  Leadership of Sparta and Athens among the Greeks.
  Love of independence (Sparta, Athens, Asia Minor).

Special Athenian Characteristics displayed.
  Generous sympathy with Greece.
  Unselfish patriotism (conduct of generals).
  Unshrinking courage.

Special Spartan Character shown.
  Strict observance of law (refusal to march).

STUDY ON PERSIAN WARS.

INTERVAL FROM FIRST TO SECOND PERSIAN WARS, MARKED BY —

Development of Athenian Naval Power, through
    wisdom of Themistocles.
    patriotism of the Athenians.
    natural advantages of Athenian situation.

Persian Preparations for invading Greece
    urged on by
        Persian desire for revenge.
        Pisistratid ambition.
    marked by
        union of great masses under single lead.
        lack of any inspiration of patriotism.
        difficulty of provisioning.

Attempted Union of Hellenes, incomplete through
    jealousy (Syracuse, Argos).
    fear (Corcyra).

Nobility of Athenian Spirit, shown in
    patriotism for *all* Hellas (Pan-Hellenism).
    generosity of Themistokles to Aristeides.
    hoping against hope, — courage in extremity.

SECOND PERSIAN WAR.

[Add to the table of "Comparison of Antagonists" the point of "Spirit," — the Hellenic spirit being that of independence, giving strength; the Persian, that of servility and fear, producing weakness.]

Causes of War (see second point under Interval).

Critical Battles of the War.
    Thermopylæ (hero *Leonidas*).
    Salamis (hero *Themistocles*).
    Platæa and Mycale.

Character displayed in this War, by —
    Spartans under Leonidas:
        · Dogged courage.
        Absolute obedience to law, and regard for religion.
        Individual independence of a leader.
    Spartans in the fleet:
        Caution and selfishness.

SECOND PERSIAN WAR. — *Continued.*
    Athenians (including Themistocles and Aristides):
        Regard for the gods.
        Good judgment (statesmanship).
        Strategy (Themistocles).
        Unselfish patriotism (Aristides, Platæa).
        Pan-Hellenic interest.
    Greeks in general:
        Regard for the gods.
        Love of independence.
        Tendencies to local and party jealousies.
        Regard for Sparta and Athens as leaders.
        Consciously united by
            religion (Delphi).
            speech.
            blood.
        Led by persuasion.
    Persian hosts:
        Cowardice.
        Dependence on leaders and on fear (scourge).

In the previous studies, we have seen the development of the Spartan and Athenian constitutions into their completed forms; in the Persian wars, we see these completed forms at work, acting in large and various circumstances. Up to this point, the aim of our work has been thoroughly to understand forms; now it must be thoroughly to feel the spirit, the life which animates them; furthermore, to note how far they meet, and when they fail to meet the needs of the hour. Perhaps beyond all else, it should be noted that both Athenian and Spartan constitutions were good primarily because they were worked, by a mass indeed, but by a mass composed of intelligent, self-reliant, patriotic individuals. We admire the heroism of the Spartans at Thermopylæ, the patriotism of the Athenians in voting that their public moneys should be expended in a fleet, and again and again we marvel at the excellent judgment and courage shown in the decisions of the Greek assemblies; but we must always remind the pupil that while the free constitution called forth the powers of the citizen, the intelligence of the citizen gave the free constitution power. To enforce the point, let the student but once imagine that the Athenian Ecclesia was composed of ignorant, selfish men, many of them resident in Attica only for a year or two, and he will see at once that under such circumstances, the free constitution, acting in a time of war and danger, when the state demands the highest courage and the greatest sacrifices, may become a source of positive injury. Further, let him note that when the Clisthenean arrangement of Strategi was tested for the first time at Marathon, this part of the constitution would have failed entirely had it not been for the generosity of Aristides and his companions, joined to the wisdom and daring of Miltiades. Again, the advantage which the ostracism gave, in uniting the forces of the state under a single lead, depended for its value on the good sense of each Athenian citizen and his readiness to submit to law. Other instances will be seen throughout the period. In short, the working power of the Greek constitutions depended on the fact that they were worked by men, quick-witted, generous-hearted; every unit counted one. Throughout the study it must be kept in mind that the whole theory of Greek political life was, that *persuasion*, the moving of men's thoughts and feelings by reasons and motives, is the only legitimate force by which either men or measures are lifted into leadership.

Although during the Persian wars, the individuality of the various states stood strongly forth in distinct and local colors, yet it is to this period that we owe the first appearance of that political form so interesting to all Americans, — the union of independent states for concerted action in affairs of common interest. The Amphictyonies were religious in their motive, and the old Homeric league of chiefs in the Trojan war was perhaps too unconscious and informal to be reckoned as political. But during the Persian wars, we find the Greek states, under the urging power of Athens, striving, though weakly and with ill-success, to form a true Pan-Hellenic union against the Barbarian. The want of centralization must have been strongly felt when fighting against a foe, whose greatest strength lay in his ability to handle masses simply and easily from an absolute, though despotic centre. The value of this power of centralized force in time of war should be as thoroughly understood as circumstances permit, and receives fine illustrations from the risks which the Greeks ran from disunion in the second Persian war, notably at Salamis. In this power lies the strength of despotisms; in its lack, the weakness of free governments, unless for a time they know how to subject and consolidate themselves under a single will. It is interesting to note, also, in this connection, that Delphi became a more thoroughly acknowledged centre of Greek affairs, and in some cases was even recognized as able to hold the various states responsible for a common agreement.

At the close of the whole study on the Persian wars it will be well to call attention to the fact that the great deeds, that the great results of this period, were due entirely to moral and intellectual forces; that the disastrous and complete defeat suffered by the Greeks at Thermopylæ became through its moral grandeur, not only a glory but an inspiration; and that the one state in Greece which displayed these qualities in the highest degree, namely Athens, not only deserved the leadership of the Hellenes, but obtained it.

The geographical advantages of Thermopylæ and Salamis are in reality the same, since on the one hand the narrowness of the mountain-pass, and on the other, the narrowness of the straits, enabled a few brave men to keep at bay a multitude, whom they could only encounter a few at a time.

Suggestions for Essay and Examination Work. — It has always been my habit, in reaching this point in the work, to give the pupils a chance to try their own hand at the making of a tabulated summary. According to the ability and experience of the class, they can either be allowed to make it without any help or suggestion on the part of the teacher, or the principal headings may be dictated to them to fill out. In either case, the teacher should be exceedingly careful not to hold his students to any rigid form, but to allow as wide differences of arrangement as the "logic of events" allows. The following topics and questions are suggestive: —

STUDY ON THE ATHENIAN LEADERSHIP.

What changes did the Persian wars produce in Hellas? Were they a good or an evil? Was Aristeides or Themistokles the better citizen? (Debate.) The military strength of goodness, as illustrated in these wars. Why is courage a cardinal virtue? Persia *v.* Greece. The citizen *v.* the subject. The comparative influence of the aims of glory and wealth on character. The story of a soldier at Marathon; at Thermopylæ. "I perceive that, in all things, ye are too superstitious." Journal of an Athenian citizen, 480–479 B.C. Why should the Greeks call "*Persuasion*" a goddess? The Greek victory at Thermopylæ.

D. STUDY ON THE ATHENIAN LEADERSHIP; AGE OF PERICLES; 479–431.

In dealing with the age of Pericles, it is generally too much ignored that we are studying, after all, the development of Athens alone; and while for the time being it seems to concentrate all Hellenic history within its own walls, yet it is but a single city among the Greeks. Hence, in the following tabulation, it has seemed best to emphasize this fact by considering Hellas in general, as well as Athens. No part of this summary should be given until all the work on the Athenian Leadership has been discussed; and if the students have sufficient ability, it may be well here also to ask them to tabulate their own results.

THE ATHENIAN LEADERSHIP; AGE OF PERICLES.

Organization of
    Hellas in general:
        Local self-governing cities, with attempts at Hellenic union
            in Confederacy of Delos (maritime dominion).
            in Spartan leadership (continental dominion).
    Athens:
        Completed democracy at home, with tendencies to demagogism.
        Imperialism abroad, under lead of
            Cimon.
            Pericles.

The Athenian Leadership. — *Continued.*

Characteristics of Period in
  Hellas in general:
    Party strife within cities.
      Aristocrats favored by Sparta.
      Democrats favored by Athens.
    Jealousy of cities, notably of Athens, leading to
      Peloponnesian War.
    Development of Athenian leadership by
      superior naval force.
      Pan-Hellenic spirit.
      literary and artistic supremacy.
    Development of Athenian empire by
      neglect and indifference of allies.
      Athenian ambition and strength.
  Athens:
    Development of trade and wealth.
    Development of arts, in original (Greek) directions.
      Sculpture } Parthenon.
      Architecture }
      Drama, —
        Æschylus.
        Sophocles.
        Euripides.
    General intelligence and patriotism shown in
      use of public money (Parthenon).
      character of drama and popular amusements.
      leading men of the state, —
        Aristides.
        Cimon.
        Pericles.
    Development of philosophy, — natural science, mental and moral philosophy, theology.
    Growth and influence of oratory.
    Ideals, — statesman and general, poet, philosopher, orator, good citizen; *or*
    Ideal character, — cultured, brave, genial, patriotic, eloquent.
    Production of great men, — Pericles, Socrates, Aristides, etc.

Existence of religious parties, —
   Liberal thinkers (Socrates).
   Orthodox Greeks (his prosecutors); *or*
Growth of free thought, endangering the state, —
   Trial of Socrates.

The instant the Persian wars are over, we find that the Hellenic world has widened, that its movements are larger, its wars and alliances farther-reaching than before. This is seen at once in the feeling that Sestos and Byzantium are keys to the Greek world, and as such should be so held by Greeks as to prevent any repetition of the invasions of Darius and Xerxes. But it is seen most largely in the fact that from this time on, the Greek cities tend to appear in groups, under the lead of one or another. During this period, of course, it was the Athenian group that led; in the beginning, the Confederacy of Delos was a free league of the older Greek type, in which Athens was simply the first among equals; but a most noteworthy change soon occurred, in that the chief bond of union became that of a common *interest*. Again, this league was formed, not to meet a special crisis, but to carry out a settled purpose of conscious Hellenic union; from this point of view, it was necessary that the members should be held responsible to some single member, or some central body. Hence, after the treasury was transferred to Athens, and the allies gradually allowed themselves to pay a money-tax, instead of performing active personal duties, we find them becoming uneasy, and the stress of present danger over, Athens was compelled to hold them together by main force. Hence the Greek world became undermined by party strife, mutual jealousy, and dislike, until the " logic of events " drove the states upon the Peloponnesian War. Yet, while the Confederacy of Delos failed of achieving a Greek political union, it must not be forgotten that it proved effective for the time being, in making the Ægean thoroughly Greek throughout its coasts and islands. Nor must it be forgotten that Athens, at this time purely democratic, and under the most democratic leaders, was able to carry out a foreign policy as energetic and decisive as any despot. Only to the mind of Pericles does it seem to have occurred that it might be possible to apply the *representative principle* to Greek affairs in general, and so to form a democratic union of states as well as one of citizens.

While the list of great men and works shows very positively that Athens was the intellectual centre of Hellas, and that the Greek genius culminated in her free citizens, it also shows that the whole Greek world was pervaded by the same intellectual and artistic impulses; and that these impulses always played about Greek forms and themes, so that the Greek history, mythology, and life, became the inspiration of the Greek art.

Not only does a state express its own peculiar genius by original works of art, but also in living characters. Thus Leonidas and Themistocles were as distinctively products of Greek life, as the Venus of Melos or the Parthenon. In Athenian history many such *type-characters* have been preserved for us with all the freshness of their living deeds and words; and of these, two predominate, — Pericles and Socrates. Pericles is, however, more typically Athenian, having the versatility which enabled him to be at once general, admiral, orator, statesman, scholar, artist, and gentleman. This versatility was rendered effective by a persistent will, a diligent use of time, and an upright character. His mode of life and habits of thought, his tastes and desires, were all Athenian, and thus he was chosen, year after year, as its representative man by the Athenian Ecclesia. He had moderation, wit, spirit, and, above all, that spherical development of the whole man, which he himself described (p. 106) as typically Athenian. If desired, the teacher may make some such tabulation as follows for the facts concerning Pericles: —

> **Advantages of Pericles for Leadership.**
> Honorable birth.
> Athenian training.
> Dignity of manner.
> Versatile tastes.
> Intellectual and oratorical talent.

Noble character, —
    upright.
    economical.
    firm.
    religious, without superstition.
    patriotic, public-spirited.
    merciful, kind.

Means used by Pericles to acquire Leadership.
Improvements wrought by Pericles.

Although Socrates did not, like Pericles, gather up in his own person all the tendencies and influences of the Athenian history and culture, still he represents the culmination of one set of these tendencies and influences, and probably could not have lived and worked sympathetically with so large and enthusiastic a following at any other time or place. The long course of Greek thought, which had dealt from the time of Homer with the larger problems of the destiny of man, the nature of the Deity, and the relation of each to the other and the external world, produced its consummate flower in the words and character of Socrates. Socrates may fairly be called a Pagan Christian, since we find in him not only the belief in a Deity who rules our lives, who can be reached by prayer, and who rewards the good and punishes the evil-doer, but also in him we find the hope of immortality, and, above all, the clear perception that the highest and most worthy life of man is spiritual, and that purity, truth, and obedience to the gods are the noblest aims of existence. This being the teaching of Socrates, it has often seemed strange that he should have been deemed worthy of death by the Athenians. But, if we have hitherto interpreted Greek history aright, the pupil will readily see that, in the Athenian state, religious unity was essential to political, and that any freedom of thought which would tend to free men from allegiance to that oldest and strongest of Greek political bonds, the tribal and national faith, must seem fatal to the firmness of the state. Here we have a grave political reason, which must have seemed plausible to the Athenians of that day, for the condemnation of Socrates; the more plausible, since the number of his sympathizers, judging from the votes cast, must have included a very large minority of the Athenian citizens.

It may be said that this study of Socrates is misplaced, since, in point of time, he belongs in the period of the Peloponnesian War. This fact caused me to hesitate before placing him with the men of the age of Pericles; but, on the whole, he seemed properly to belong with that great group, each of which represents the culmination of a long "stream of tendency." For a similar reason, though more doubtfully applied, the extracts from Aristophanes are placed among those illustrative of this age.

The extracts from the dramatists, taken in connection with the trial of Socrates and the life of Pericles, indicate that, in the refined Athens of that age, there were three distinct trends of religious thought: that of orthodoxy, or the holding by the material myth and the material faith; that of skepticism or doubt; and that of philosophic theology, personified in Socrates. That the third of these tendencies was regarded as more dangerous than the second may be easily explained by the fact that a positive, earnest belief has a strength which mere doubt can never possess.

I am sorry that the necessary limit set at present to the expense of a text-book has made it impossible to illustrate more fully or perfectly the culmination of Greek art into sculpture and architecture. But with the specimens given, it may be noted that its products were simple, natural, well-proportioned and harmonious, full of living repose.

Suggestions for Essay and Examination Work. — The greatness of Pericles. The greatness of Socrates. What can the Parthenon tell us of Athens? The Periclean *v.* The American. Indifference a political vice in a republic. The education of the Ecclesia. "Inspiration comes only to the disciplined"; illustrate from Athenian history and biography. The imperfections of the Athenian democracy. The political value of morality, illustrated from Athenian history and biography. The visit of an Egyptian to Athens under Pericles. Pericles *v.* Pisistratus.

E. F. STUDY ON PERIOD 431–338.

The studies on pp. 115, 117, and 118 may be summarized as follows : —

PELOPONNESIAN WAR, AND FALL OF GREECE BEFORE MACEDON.

Characteristics of Period.
  Dependence of individual states on foreign aid.
    Persia.
    Macedon.
  Succession of Hellenic leaderships, or leagues, under
    Athens, — caused by naval and intellectual superiority.
    Sparta, — caused by superior military strength and foreign aid.
    Thebes, — caused by native patriotism and culture.
    Macedon, — caused by royal ambition, interference in Greek affairs, diplomacy.
  Mutual jealousies and constant wars.
  Gradual weakening of important states through
    lack of union (fault in organization).
    lack of Hellenic patriotism and local unselfishness (fault in spirit).

General Characteristics of Hellenic History.
  Local individual development from common Homeric basis:
    Of constitutions, into tyrannies, democracies, aristocracies.
    Of ideals, into statesmen, generals, poets, artists, philosophers.
    Of religion, into Socratic philosophy, popular superstition.

The opening of the Peloponnesian War shows us the Greek world in all its relations within and without : two strong groups of states within, engaged in a long-threatened conflict, and representing the opposing principles of aristocracy and democracy as embodied in their leading cities ; these cities gradually weakened and deserted by their allies, the strength of their respective confederacies broken, and passing, in some measure, to Thebes; meanwhile, the relation toward the barbarian had so far changed that Persia was enabled to interfere very effectively in Greek affairs, the Greek bitterness towards her being very materially softened. The Persian sympathy was naturally at first against Athens, who had proved her most dangerous and persistent foe in the Persian wars; but when Athens was weakened, the Asiatics attacked Sparta, and the whole Greek world was undermined by mutual jealousy and foreign intrigue. Philip of Macedon, therefore, found it comparatively easy to follow the lead of Persia, and to develop still further that policy of aiding one Greek state against another to the mutual injury or ruin of both, while he himself held all his forces in his single hand, to obey his single will. If Athens had had the spirit to follow the lead of Demosthenes, and Greece the spirit to follow the one lead of Athens; or if, in the preceding generation, Pericles had been able to form that Hellenic Union, which the best Athenians desired, then Greece might have become the leading power of the Eastern Mediterranean. But the maritime power of Athens had been thoroughly broken at Ægospotami, and with it her power of holding her old allies; the influence of Persian gold was strong in Sparta and the smaller Grecian states; neither the spirit nor the organization existed capable of resisting such a power as Philip possessed. For Philip possessed not only material powers, such as Persia held; but by becoming a Greek unto the Greeks, he was able to *disguise their national subjection under national sympathies and forms.* His wars were Greek wars, in which he led Greek against Greek, and even at the fatal day of Chæronea, it was as an elected general of Greek forces that he subdued the last independent cities; and when he called a Hellenic congress at Corinth, and was chosen captain-general of Hellenic forces against the Asiatic, there must have been many of the Greeks who believed that their race was just about to enter on a still greater career.

From the siege of Troy to the day of Chæronea, the course of Greek history is clearly evolutional and singularly free from outside influence. In politics, from first to last, the constant tendency to Hellenic union is overborne by the stronger tendency to local independence. This latter tendency, of course, had its advantage, in that it gave each local character opportunity to develop itself completely and distinctly. Each Homeric ideal culminates in the fifth century B.C.; — Achilles into the Spartan warrior ideal; Ulysses into the Athenian who is at once general and statesman; the bard has grown through generations to the full stature of the Athenian dramatists. That these types tended to culminate so variously in Athens is to be attributed, perhaps, mainly to two facts: one, her free trading and commercial life, which took her citizens to and fro through the contemporaneous world, quickening their minds with new ideas, enlarging their hearts with new sympathies; the other, her free constitution, which educated every man to hear, to think, to decide in regard to matters of larger import than the petty round of merely individual life can furnish.

Suggestions for Dictation and Examination. — Illustrate from Greek history the saying, "He who will save his life shall lose it." The military value of unselfishness. We say now-a-days, "The pen is mightier than the sword"; what would an Athenian have said instead, and how might he have illustrated it? When did the fall of Greece begin, and how? Why should Athenians be quicker to seize opportunity than the Spartans? Why should they be more patriotic than Persians? Than other Greeks? Why should they be more interested in Greece as a whole than other Greeks were? What had made the Athenians, as a whole, politically acute? Demosthenes v. Philip. The real causes of the Peloponnesian War. Its results and effects. Letters of an Athenian to a Milesian, 405–338. The Spartan v. the Athenian spirit. Influence of the Greek ideas and ideals in our own time.

THE HELLENISTIC OR ALEXANDRIAN CONQUESTS AND KINGDOMS, 338–146 B.C.

The general results of the work on pp. 119–127 may be summarized as follows: —

THE HELLENISTIC OR ALEXANDRIAN CONQUESTS AND KINGDOMS.

Organizations formed.
  Military monarchies or despotisms, supported by standing armies.

Results of Conquests and the Foundation of the New Kingdoms.
  Development of trade.
    New trade-routes opened to the East:
      Canal from Nile to Red Sea.
      Trading posts in Indian Ocean.
    Foundation of new trade-centres:
      Alexandria.
      Antioch.
      Seleucia (near Babylon).
      Pergamos.
  Development of art, science, and literature, in new directions, with Alexandria, Antioch, and Pergamos, as centres.
    Natural science, especially
      medicine.
      astronomy.
      physics.
    Poetry, — pastoral and elegiac.
    Drama, — new comedy.
  Spread of Greek language, in Egypt, Macedon, Syria, Asia Minor, and eastward toward India.

Character of Civilization (Hellenistic) affected by previous Egyptian and Oriental culture.
  Dependent on courts for development and support.
  Practical in its tendencies, seen in
    new schools of ethics, —
      Epicureanism.
      Stoicism.

> new forms of literature, —
>> new comedy.
>> pastoral and ⎱ poetry.
>> elegiac ⎰
>
> new directions of thought, —
>> scientific.

It should be distinctly felt that the conquests of Alexander owe their importance to the fact that they were the conquests of Hellenism; by Hellenism, meaning the spirit of Hellenic culture, rather than its body. For it will be seen that the Alexandrian art, poetry, thought, and activity, ran after all in new channels, determined by the contact of the versatile Hellenic mind with new circumstances and with old, firmly-fixed civilizations, fitted rather to give than receive impressions. The spirit of local patriotism yielded to the cosmopolitanism of an empire; and the seriousness of Socrates, Æschylus, and Aristophanes, changed to the practical observations and ethics of men of the world. That Alexander felt and made himself the representative of the Greek world is clear enough; chosen general-in-chief of Greek forces by a congress of Hellenic states, sanctioned by Delphi, sacrificing to the Greek deities, dedicating his spoils to the Athena of the Acropolis, and establishing Greek political forms in the cities he founded and conquered, the pupil of Aristotle and the lover of Homer seemed to be Greek in all but name.[1] That the Greeks themselves were uneasy under the Alexandrian rule militates not in the least against this view, since throughout their organization and history, their little city-states were always uneasy under any attempt at centralization, whether native or foreign; and during this very period, we find their most hopeful attempts at political union, the Greek leagues, — the famous forerunners of modern confederacies such as are our United States, — marred by their partial character; while all the attempts to regain

---

[1] It is interesting to note in this connection the modern Greek claim to the old Macedonian land, as a just part of the Greek territory.

independence are too local to have the least worth. In fact, the whole Greek history is an illustration of *particularism*, a term which the teacher may do well to introduce as the antithesis of centralization.

It will be noted in the progressive history of the Aryan world that states and empires increase in size; thus, the Alexandrian empire exceeds the Persian in this respect, and is itself exceeded by the Roman. This Alexandrian empire illustrates, too, both in its conquests and its foundations, the fact that the ancient world was held and characterized by its great metropolitan centres of wealth, population, and art. It was not the desire of land that drew Alexander eastward with his Greeks; the heaped-up splendors of Tyre and Sidon, of Jerusalem and Damascus, of Memphis and Babylon, were richer booty than the rough North and West could offer, and their possession meant the absolute possession of all their subject lands; since without their walls was neither wealth, nor will, nor leadership for resistance; the land was but their great dumb feeder. So to establish his own power permanently, Alexander felt that he must found cities, that should stamp and rule all the surrounding land and folk; hence, the noble foundations of Alexandria, Antioch, Pergamos, Candahar, Smyrna, enduring, living monuments of Hellenistic sagacity and power. But from this very fact of strong and widely separated centres, the Alexandrian empire, though continuous in territory and with the same governing people, could not hold together. The interests of each centre were too strong and too strongly supported by old historic divisions of language, faith, and spirit, to allow of anything more than the most fleeting union. Of these new foundations, Alexandria is justly considered greatest, since it commanded the commerce of the Nile, and all the caravan routes of Southern Asia. In our own times, it has gained a new importance by the opening of the Suez Canal.

Since Alexander is of the small number whom all men call "Great," it will be wise for the teacher to dwell on the force of the adjective as here applied; of course Alexander's work was great since it effected the union of the Greek and Orient worlds; but that the man himself was great is shown by the very facts of his eastward march; by the net of conquest which he drew about Asia Minor, by securing all the strong cities of her coasts, thus holding the outlets and inlets of the country; by the courage and perseverance with which he pushed across hostile, desert, and unknown lands, to discover what and where the wonderland of India was; by the unbroken daring with which, in the face of mutiny, he built a fleet in order to send Nearchus back a new way; by the boundless energy and wisdom with which he dotted his march with towns.

Suggestions for Essay and Examination Work. — Was Alexander the Conqueror or the Representative of the Greeks? (Debate.) Journal of a Greek soldier in the Alexandrian army. Letter of a discontented Macedonian soldier from an Indian encampment. The debt of civilization to the Alexandrian despots. Alexander compared with Xerxes. The advantages and disadvantages of individualism as illustrated by Greek history. Compare the Greek invasion of Asia with the Asiatic invasion of Greece. The influence of the Orient on Greek thought and action in Alexandrian times.

ROME, 753 (?) B.C. – 800 A.D.

The answers to the questions on p. 130 may be summarized as follows: —

ITALY.

Geographic Character and Position.
    Large, fertile plains, with easy, natural separations:
        Valley of the Po.
        Plains eastward of the Apennines.
        Plains of Campania.
    Variety of soil and production.
    Protection from invasion by
        Alps.
        Seas.

Italy. — *Continued.*
    Central position in Mediterranean, commanding commerce of Spain, the Rhone valley, the African coasts, and all eastern commerce passing by it westward.[1]
    Nearest civilized neighbors at 776 B.C.:
        Carthage (Phœnician).
        Greece.

Race Distribution, determined by mountain barriers and river-basins.
    Kelts, in Po valley.
    Italians and Etruscans, in centre.
        Latins, centred about Rome.
        Samnites, in mountains.
        Etruscans, in Tuscan plain.
    Greeks, in south and in Sicily.

Results of Geographic Character and Position of Italy.
    Natural political divisions larger than in Greece.
    Beginning of civilization later than in Greece.
    Natural occupation and support, —
        agriculture and commerce.
    Sources of foreign civilization, —
        Greek and Phœnician.

Special Advantages of Rome.
    Central position in Italy.
    Commands the Tiber water-way.
    Unites seven hill-fortresses.
    In the midst of a fertile plain.

While the geographical advantages and peculiarities of Italy should be clearly appreciated, too much stress must not be laid upon them, since all history teaches that while geography is a great primary factor in *starting* a people, it soon becomes overlaid and involved with many other factors as powerful, so that, in time, it loses much of its influence.

---

[1] Of course this command would only come with the mastery of Italy and Sicily by a single power; this acquired, Italy is easily mistress of all the Mediterranean commerce passing her eastward or westward, by virtue of the narrow seas between herself and Africa.

A. B. I. STUDY ON REGAL ROME AND PRÆ-PUNIC REPUBLIC.

The studies, pp. 130–151 inclusive, may be summarized somewhat as follows : —

REGAL AND PRÆ-PUNIC REPUBLICAN ROME.

Organizations of the Period within (Roman).
    Patrician monarchy.
        Power centred in a king, limited by a body of patricians, bound together by *birth* and *worship*, 753(?)–510(?) B.C.
    Patrician aristocratic republic, 510(?) B.C.
        Developed by patrician revolt against the oppression of royalty in
            concentrating power.
            in use of public money.
            imposition of public burdens.
        Based on bonds of kinship and religion.
        Characterized by
            concentration of power in hands of senate.
            division of royal power among magistrates.
    Patricio-plebeian republic, 264 B.C.
        Developed by party strife of patricians and plebeians, caused by
            social and } class distinctions.
            political }
            harsh debt-laws.
            unjust distribution of land.
        strengthened by
            military power of plebeians.
            traditional and organized rule of patricians.
        neutralized by
            common interest and needs in
                defence and
                conquest.
        Based on bonds of common interest and residence.
    Rigid social classes (patricians, plebeians)
        formed by distinctions of birth and worship.
        distinguished by exclusive patrician privileges.

REGAL AND PRÆ-PUNIC REPUBLICAN ROME. — *Continued.*
    composed of patriarchal families, forming clans and tribes, as with the Greeks.

Organizations of Period without (Italian).
  The Roman military and agricultural colony.
  The Latin league.
  The Italian allied towns.

Developments and Tendencies of People and Time.
  Democracy.
    Equal distribution of political power.
  Social equality.
  Political parties.
    Patricians *v.* plebeians.
    Rich *v.* poor (compare with aristocrats and democrats, the Eupatrids and the "Many" of the Greek cities).
  Constant and consolidated growth of dominion.
    Caused by
      order of conquest, —
        Latium, Etruria.
        Samnium.
        South Italy.
      mixture of Romans and Italians in
        residence.
        religion.
        government and law.
      superiority of Rome to neighboring peoples in
        defences.
        position.
        organization.
    Resulting in uniting Italy in
      language (Latin).
      law, habits, religion.
  Introduction of foreign culture (from Greece and Phœnicia).
  Original development in
    architecture, —
      arch.
    government, —
      constitution of Rome.
      management of conquests.

Characteristics of Period.

> Close union of politics and religion (church and state).
> Polytheistic faith.
> Utilitarianism, seen in
> > religion.
> > public works.
> > attitude towards art and literature.
>
> Domination of individual by state.
> Strict regard for form and order, seen in
> > politics.
> > religion.
>
> Patrician dignity, pride, patriotism.
> Severity and simplicity, seen in
> > law.
> > manners.
> > style of life, —
> > > agricultural.
> > > military.
>
> Ideals of period, —
> > warrior.
> > law-giver.
> > farmer.

Just here, in the study of the Roman constitutions, the teacher will find the advantage of having taken time for the thorough understanding of the constitutional development of Athens; if this has been mastered, he will find that the work on the development of the Roman constitution may be made little more than a quick review and application of what the pupil already knows. For, although more complex and extended, the constitutions of Rome are, after all, of the antique type, and follow from stage to stage the antique development. As in the Athenian, so in the Roman state, these marked revolutions occur. Within an original society, composed of the king and his tribal nobles, known as Eupatrids or Patricians ("the well-born," the "fathers"), the oppressions of the king, and the power of the nobles, result in the overthrow of monarchy, and the establishment of a state, exclusive and aristocratic to the outside world, but within itself pervaded with political and social equality. This aristocratic republic, in turn attacked by those without its pale of birth and worship, is compelled little by little to yield a place and name in the state, to the real powers of wealth, labor, plebeian numbers and fighting value, until at last, a final stage is reached by the constitutions of Clisthenes, and the Patricio-Plebeian Republic, in which all dwellers in the state are citizens endowed, by law at least, with equal powers and rights.

While this is the general course of the development of the ancient state, attention should be called to more detailed comparisons; as that the Roman *curies* correspond to the old Ionic tribes of the time of Solon; that the *centuries* are divided like the Solonian tribes according to wealth; while the *tribes* of 264 B.C. are the Roman equivalent for the tribes of Clisthenes; again, the division of the people into adverse parties on account of distinctions of birth and wealth, and oppressive laws of debt, is duplicated from the Hellenic cities. It is well, also, to allow the pupil to foretell the probable changes in the Roman state from Greek analogies as well as from the actual Roman conditions; thus, he should be able to foresee from both points of view, that the first revolution will result in the transference of power from the king to the nobles. Here too, as strictly as in Sparta, the military organization was identical with the political; a fact which enabled the evidently large plebeian population of Rome to win its way into the state as its necessary defenders.[1] This hold which the plebeians had upon the patricians is well illustrated by the story from Livy on p. 136, which admirably shows the temper of either party, — the plebeian impatience of patrician lordship, the patrician fear of plebeian desertion, — while we see both impatience and fear first yield-

---

[1] This is by no means a necessary relation, except in states of the military type; in industrial communities, workers are worth as much as soldiers to the state.

ing before the pressing need of defending their common city, and then culminating in the affair of the Sacred Mount, by which the fixed determination of the plebeians gained a place in the magistracy of the city, in spite of the obstinate tenacity of the nobles.

The characteristic features in the growth of Rome's dominion are best seen in contrast with the imperial growth of Athens; Athens stands as a single city among equals who consent to follow her leadership; the one word that expresses the power and character of Roman rule is unity; Rome peoples her subject lands with her citizens; her colonies are no commercial outposts of traders who always remember they are Greeks among barbarians; they are communities of soldier-farmers, who seize and settle the land, become "sons of the soil," and little by little force upon the people their own standards of law and faith and speech, through the power of their fixed and dominant relation.

After the studies on the constitution and the dominion of Rome, the pupils are fairly ready to understand the historical force of the words " growth " and " development "; the former applying exactly to the increase in size of the state, while the latter describes the unfolding of its various parts or organs to their complete relations and force.

In studying the life, the art, the works of Rome, it is apparent that whatever is of use in the house or the farm, in the camp or the forum, is accepted and admired, and that any superfluous thing is rejected as effeminate; in their assemblies, men are expected to vote independently and decisively, without listening to discussions or speeches which might sway their minds; the native art hardly goes further than to commemorate a great deed by a tablet, or a great man by an attempt at a portrait-statue, or to build a mighty wall against invasion; hence, so far as it goes, that art has the mere stamp of simplicity and effective strength. Even in their faith, the gods are evidently regarded first of all as powers whose favor it is well to gain by prayer and sacrifice and festival, because they can give plentiful harvests and abundant victory; the deities, like the folk, live and move and have their being in the visible working circle of the hearth, the field, the tent, the forge.

Better than anything else, the Twelve Tables reflect the temper of that early Roman polity; absolute justice and equality among citizens; protection for the very slave of Rome; but for the outsider, the "foreigner," no law, no recognition; even for the citizen, no escape from the rigors of the harshest penalty; the state dominates all; here, as in a mirror, we see the stern, harsh life of the warlike, superstitious, exclusive, strong-handed city.

Suggestions for Essay and Examination Work. — Geographic influence on Roman character. Comparison of Roman and Athenian environment; same of development. Roman character as seen in Roman faith. Speech of a plebeian to his fellows on the Sacred Mount. Visit of an Athenian to Rome about 400 B.C. Same of a Spartan. The gods of Greece *versus* the gods of Rome. How far was Rome a civilized state at 264 B.C.? Pericles and Cincinnatus. What was the use of a dictator to Rome?

B. II. STUDY ON REPUBLICAN ROME, PUNIC PERIOD.

In the study on the Punic period the military type of state is brought sharply into contrast with the commercial type; this one fact marks the difference, — Rome conquers her neighbors, while Carthage pays them tribute. This by no means says that the Romans were the braver folk, but simply that their living was partly dependent on war, and the gains of war, while for theirs, the Carthaginians demanded leisure, and friendly relations with as many peoples as possible.

The studies on pp. 153, 155, 158, 162, 164, 166, 169, may be summarized something as follows: —

PUNIC PERIOD, 264-146 B.C. — ROME AGAINST CARTHAGE.

Comparative View of Antagonists, 264 B.C.

	Rome.	Carthage.
Territory:	Continental, — Italy, south of Apennines.	Maritime; colonial,—Sicily, African and west Mediterranean coasts, Spain (Cadiz), Sardinia.
Armies:	Citizens.	Mercenaries, and subject peoples.
Basis of life, occupation:	Agriculture.	Commerce.
Material civilization:[1]	Primitive.	Highly developed.
Ideal:	Soldier and law-giver.	Wealthy merchant and skilful navigator.

Comparative Power among states, — about equal, as shown by the affair of the Mamertines.

Growth of Rome during Period.
    In dominion.
        By First Punic War, —
            Sicily, Corsica, Sardinia, alliances in Spain and Gaul.
        By Second Punic War, —
            Spain, dependent alliance of Carthaginian Africa.
        By period from Second to Third Punic War, —
            Cisalpine Gaul.
            Macedonia and Greece.
            Western Asia Minor.
        By Third Punic War, —
            Carthaginian Africa, as a province.

[Note that this conquest is *steady* and *progressive*, new possessions being adjacent to old.]
    In wealth:
        The tribute of Carthage, Macedonia, and Sicily.
    In fighting power:
        Tributary troops of Carthage, Macedonia, and Sicily;

---

[1] After the preliminary study on Phœnicia, this comparison should be made almost without thinking on the part of the student.

Punic Period, 264-146 b.c. — *Continued.*
>> Allied troops of Western Asia;
>> The formation of a fleet; ∴
>> Becomes leading military power of Mediterranean.
> In influence:
>> Becomes leader and arbiter of Mediterranean lands.
> In organization:
>> Beginning of provincial governments (*imperial type*).
> In civilization:
>> Influence of Greece and the Orient, seen in
>>> literature.
>>> art.
>>> life.

Character displayed during Period.
> By Carthage:
>> Avarice, — mistaken prudence; at the last, patriotism.
>> Dependence on great generals, and their personal power over mercenaries (*Hannibal*).[1]
> By Hannibal:
>> Patriotism, perseverance, determination, ingenuity, courage, personal power, good judgment.
> By Greece:
>> Disunion, jealousy, love of freedom.
> By Rome, before the close of Second Punic War:
>> Reliance on whole body of citizens, on law and patriotism.
>> Patriotism, determination, courage, perseverance.
>> Strong regard for religious forms.
>> Native genius, — military, legal, engineering.
>> Concentration of life at city of Rome:
>>> Legal and military, in hands of patricians.
>>> Literary and artistic, in hands of foreigners (Greeks).

---

[1] Note that Hannibal's single qualities, acting through a body of loyal soldiery, match the collective qualities of the Roman state, acting through a body of patriotic citizens. Hannibal has within himself those elements of success which Rome possesses, and which Carthage lacks; but finally, he lacks the independent power to develop his own genius to a victorious issue. It is a significant contrast that Carthage concentrates her greatness in a single man, while Rome obtains greatness from the diffusion of great qualities among her citizens.

By Rome, in later Punic period, 201-146 B.C.
    Growth of new aristocracy on bases of
        military ⎫
        official ⎬ superiority.
        monied ⎭
    Tendency to subject law to the individual (Scipio, Fabius).
    Growth of demagogism, — games, corn distributions.
    Growth of popular power (Roman rabble).
    Political corruption.
    Harshness, cruelty, and injustice to allies, provincials, and slaves.
    Influx of Greek and Oriental culture
        brought in by
            triumphs.
            returning soldiers and officials.
        opposed by Cato and old-style Romans.
    Ideal, — the successful general with plenty of booty.
    Taste for coarse and cruel amusements, — low comedy, gladiatorial fights.
    Tendencies to atheism, together with superstition and formality.
    Decay of small farmers
        caused by
            large estates worked by slaves, *hence*
            no demand for free labor.
            distributions of cheap or free provincial grain at Rome, *hence*
            no Roman market for grain.
        resulting in
            drift of landless men to Rome.
            selling of the suffrage.
            idle Roman populace, dependent on foreign bread.
            dangerous country population of slaves.

The chief point to be noted in regard to organization during this period is the formation of an imperial relation. This relation really begins with the acquisition of Sicily and the establishment of provincial government, personified in proconsuls, whose absolute rule abroad introduced the imperial principle into the Roman state. This point, though simple, must be emphasized, since the whole fabric of the empire had this for its excuse, the necessity of some organization by which a city could rule far-distant peoples and lands, and the emperors were always the rulers of the provinces rather than of Rome. The events of the later Punic period show very clearly how it was that when Rome had once made herself decidedly stronger than her neighbors, they naturally sought her alliance and her influence; thus, as the keeper of the peace, or as the champion of one party, people, or prince against another, the chosen arbiter and protector of the various Mediterranean lands became their administrator and conqueror. Even in this period, it is to be noted, that while the subject peoples of Rome were forced to accept absolutism at her hands, yet it was perhaps a lesser evil than their own chronic condition of civil war and anarchy. Just here, the pupil should be able to foresee something of the necessary future growth of Roman dominion, and at least to forecast the completion of the Mediterranean circle. If the teacher think best, he may at once ask for a comparison of the map on p. 157, with that of the finished empire, when the pupil will see that the natural process of growth only ends when great natural boundaries are reached, — the Rhine, the Danube, the ocean, the Sahara.

The details of the Second Punic War are remarkably instructive, since by the very nature of the case they give us a constant comparison of characters and tempers and organizations. The citizen army *versus* the mercenary band, the popular control of military movements as opposed to the absolutism of a great general, the respective play of moral forces in the industrial and the commercial state — all these are well worth studying. In the text I have called attention to a few detailed points, as to that unfortunate Roman organization which divided the command of the army between two consuls at the crisis of Cannæ, when, if ever, Rome needed the absolute rule of a dictator to ensure prompt decision and consistency of action.

The teacher will find it well worth his while to *take all the time necessary* to a fair appreciation of the changed conditions of Roman life and the consequent change in Roman character that are found in existence in the later Punic period, since thoroughness here means the easy comprehension of the Empire. The fundamental change of all is due to the new ideals that entered the popular mind. The successful general, returning with plenty of money and with hosts of strange and beautiful objects, easily became the popular hero, and could have what he would from the admiring crowd whose man he was willing to be. He could not oppress the Roman populace, it is true, for he had competitors who might outbid him to-morrow in glory or generosity; unfortunately, competitors of his own kind, for, by that constitutional fault which Pericles found it well to correct in Athens, no poor man could afford to hold office, since public officers were unpaid.[1] Hence arose a class of men, who wrested victories and tributes from abroad to become kind, indulgent demagogues at home. Perhaps Scipio may fairly stand as the first of the line which ended only with the firm establishment of imperialism.

In the midst of her rapidly growing dominion, Rome was threatened by new dangers from within. Those arising from the oppression of slaves and allies are too evident and too temporary to require more than a simple passing notice; but the most careful attention should be given to the land-question, since it is one of our pressing modern problems, and since, in the later republic, the actual facts are so well known, and the logic of events and conditions pressed so relentlessly on to its fatal end. By the importation of foreign slaves into Italy, the market for rural labor was destroyed, since the wealthy non-resident Roman landlords found it cheaper to work their country-estates by slaves; by the importation of foreign grain, which rival demagogues cheapened or even gave away, the market for wheat was taken from the farmers of Italy, and without capital

---

[1] Compare modern constitutions, British and American.

they found themselves quite unable to compete against the masters of large slave-worked estates, as raisers of stock or keepers of vineyards. So the small country holdings and the multitudinous country interests that held the men of Italy bound in close relations to her soil gradually died out, and the country population became one of slaves, mostly imported from abroad, with no interest, native or acquired, either in the soil or its labors. As for the owners of these estates, they mostly lived at Rome, using their country places for revenue and pleasure; meanwhile, the old country population crowded to the city, where it formed an idle, helpless herd, corrupting the decisions of the Forum by its mercenary votes, sold to the highest bidder for amusement or food. Thus the living union of the soil and the man perished, the respect for labor vanished when it was no longer free, and the people of Italy became largely dependent on the provinces for food. Thus a natural relation arose between successful conquerors or rulers of provinces and successful and popular magistrates in Rome, and again the inevitable course toward imperialism was confirmed.

The last question on p. 169 calls for a classification of the dangerous tendencies of Rome into those that are politically, socially, and religiously so. But I have purposely set this question in order to call attention to the fact that it is almost impossible to make such a classification since the social, political, and religious life, all make the complex organism of the state, and are inextricably mingled in its structure. The varied classifications made by the pupils will easily elucidate this point.

Suggestions for Essay and Examination Work. — The military *versus* the industrial character. (Debate.) The debate at Messana over the Roman or Carthaginian alliance. The end of Greece. The citizen army; its defects and excellencies. The causes of the growth of the new aristocracy at Rome. When was Rome greater, at 264 or 146 B.C.? At what time would you have been proudest to have been a Roman citizen? Draw parallels between any modern conditions that you know and the condition of affairs at Rome in the later Punic period. Account of a Spanish soldier to his village-comrades of the Italian campaign with Hannibal. A Roman soldier's first visit to

Athens. What tendencies and characteristics of the later Punic period seem to you legitimate developments from the earlier Roman character?

B. III. STUDY ON REPUBLICAN ROME, POST-PUNIC PERIOD.

The work from pp. 170-192 should reach the general results indicated in the following summary: —

ROMAN REPUBLIC, POST-PUNIC PERIOD, 146-27 B.C.

Organization. — **Military, Imperial, Democratic.**
    Imperial, through the Mediterranean basin, excepting Italy.
    Democratic, in Italy, centering
        at Rome.
        in military leaders, or Imperators (*Emperors*).

Characteristics.
    Constant party strife, — over questions, over persons, between
        people and senate (democracy *v*. aristocracy).
        Italians and Romans.
        poor and rich.
    Social and political discontent
        displaying itself in
            dissensions of the Gracchi.
            servile revolts.
            Social War.
        resulting in
            agrarian laws (to check the growth of large estates).
            extension of suffrage to Italy.
    Progressive growth[1] of Roman dominion to natural limits of
        seas, rivers, mountains, deserts. (See map.)
    Progressive centralization of power
        in persons of successful generals, —
            Marius.
            Sulla.
            Pompey.
            Julius Cæsar.
            Augustus Cæsar *Imperator* (emperor).

---

[1] The easy and natural course of this progressive dominion, as compared with the long and endless civil disturbances, indicates that the real strength of Rome lay in her armies rather than in her constitutions.

ROMAN REPUBLIC. — *Continued.*

    developed by necessities of the state for
      provincial order.
      frontier defence.
      military organization.
   based on popular favor, secured by
      games, grain-distribution.
      eloquence in favor of popular measures.
      generous use of money.
      actual command of armed forces.
      military success.
  Corruption and weakness of Roman government,
    consisting in
      bribery, extortion, injustice, inefficiency, stupid selfishness (treatment of allies).
    seen in
      the Jugurthine War.
      the conspiracy of Catiline.
      the prosecution of Verres.
      constant civil wars and disturbances, and their difficult suppression.
  Growing love of wealth and pleasure.
  Development of native Italian talent
    in oratory
    in poetry (under Greek influence) } new.[1]
    in history
    in engineering, law, politics, war, — as before.
  Growth of skepticism among cultured, of superstition among masses,
    resulting in
      adoption of Greek philosophy
      deification of Cæsar.
      identification of religion with the state.

---

[1] It is to be noted that when the Italian genius began to display itself in a literature truly Latin, it still declared itself a practical genius, choosing facts and contemporary life and incident for its material, even when dependent on the Greeks for form. The direction which the native genius was to take in all its original work is well marked out by the list of subjects on which the Elder Cato wrote, p. 163.

The above tabulation is so very general that it can only be given after the full completion of the work. During its progress, the teacher may wish to sub-summarize the results of some of the special studies something as follows: —

"**Dissensions of the Gracchi.**"
    Caused by
        unequal distribution of land.
        unequal political status of Italians and Romans.[1]
        exclusive judicial power of senate.
        discontent of
            poor.
            knights.
            Italians.
    Resulting in
        formation of parties:
            Democratic (radical, reforming party, embodied in popular assembly).
            Aristocratic (conservative party, embodied in senate).
        more violent agitation (Drusus, and Social War).
        establishing of precedents of violent and illegal action in city government.

The last point in this summary is of prime importance; from the time of the Gracchi onward, neither the people nor their leaders seriously hesitated to use force or to override the constitution in order to achieve their aims. Thus Marius and Sulla ruled the Forum by force of arms, disregarded or tyrannized over elections, while Sulla, as dictator, assumed not only the powers of a general, but those of the Roman assemblies as well, in disposing of the lands and lives of citizens.

Perhaps there is no one series of events so instructive in regard to all the political relations at Rome as that of the

---

[1] The Roman franchise meant to the Italians cheap grain, a share in the conquered lands of the rapidly growing dominion of Rome, opportunity for glory, wealth, and political power. The Romans naturally delayed to grant it, since division of the spoils meant a smaller share for themselves.

Jugurthine War. At its opening, we see just how it was that Rome became so easily mistress when once she became mediator. Numidia, nominally independent, was in reality the absolute subject of Rome, and declared herself so in the alternate appeals of her princes. As soon as actual interference began, we see in turn the moral weakness of Rome, the inability of her senators and generals to maintain an acknowledged right against the power of the bribe, the insubordination of her armies, the unwillingness of her generals to displease the mob of the forum or the camp. Again we see the close relation existing between success on the field and official success in Rome, the rivalry of the Italian and the Roman, of the senate and the tribes. The whole history is not so significant as being the story of the conquest of Numidia as in being the account of the subtle ruin which Roman citizens, generals, and senators were all bringing upon their native city.

The provincial government of Verres injured Rome by diminishing her revenue, reputation, and consequent power, by wasting and depopulating her grain-growing estates, by shaking that religious faith which always formed a basis of political power in antiquity. The speech of Cicero, moreover, shows that the case of Verres was typical, and that provincial oppression and greed of provincial office for the sake of provincial spoils was no uncommon thing.

In the rise of Julius Cæsar we have another of those special studies that throw light for us on the whole contemporary life and action of the state. The prominent qualities of his character were resolution, hardihood, unscrupulousness, daring, mixed with prudence, patience, temperance, generosity, intellectual taste and power, personal vanity and ambition, warm and ready sympathies with those who aided or did not withstand his power; add to this the genius of Rome's greatest general, and an eloquence equal to that of the best, and you find combined in this one man every quality needful for success in a government fallen into the hands of a spoiled city populace, ready to be bought by the magnificent expenditures which Cæsar well knew how to make, and ready to be intimidated by troops invincibly attached to a leader who was the personification of good fellowship and soldierly quality. Fortunately for Rome, however, Cæsar was greater than a mere demagogue. He aspired not to be greater because of Rome, but to make Rome greater because of Cæsar; hence, to his name and suggestion may be traced many of the noblest measures of the early empire. The latest follower of the Gracchi, he stood for the rights of the provinces as they had stood for those of Italy. He had a higher ambition than to give the citizens of Rome new peoples for slavery and new lands for plunder; he had a vision of a strong and thoroughly-welded state, that should be comprised of provincials as well as Romans, but through which the Roman genius should interpenetrate a living growth by transmarine and transalpine colonization. Hence, we find that the enemies of Cæsar are Romans, while the universal provincial mourning for him shows the cosmopolitan sympathies which he felt and aroused. Perhaps the time has not yet passed when every one has a right to his own opinion as to the effect of Cæsar's death on Rome. To us, his assassination seems but to prolong the death-agony of the republic, and delay the inevitable birth of empire.

Throughout these studies, the constant evolutional relation between the tendencies and character of the later Punic period, and the tendencies and character of the last age of the republic should be kept in view.

The "General Study" on p. 189 should allow the freest discussion and the largest possible range of opinion, at the same time that certain positive generalizations are made, as that, from beginning to end, the Romans had one unchanging ideal, the military, and one unchanging taste, for the practical. In the later republic we see the new ideals of wealth and pleasure arising from new resources brought to Rome by her victorious armies; meanwhile, the old admiration for a simple, even severe, type of morals and manners gives way before the charms of the Greeks and the lawlessness of popular heroes. In fact, regarding the native Roman genius as practical, legal, military, the most Roman age of all her history would seem to be that of the earlier republic, culminating in the epic of the second Punic war. But here opinions would justly differ.

Suggestions for Essay and Examination Work. — What essentials for good republican government did Rome lack in the first century B.C.? Dialogue regarding their respective miseries between a Greek slave and an Italian farmer, 100 B.C. Julius Cæsar, the avenger of the Gracchi. The political importance of the murder of Tiberius Gracchus. Journal of a Roman citizen, 88–78 B.C. The popular origin of the emperors. The Greek *versus* the Roman genius. (Debate.) The relation between Roman tastes and amusements, and the development of the Roman character. Letter written home by a Gallic soldier and senator on the occasion of Cæsar's death. The Roman roads and the Roman Empire. Reflections of Adherbal on Rome. Reflections of Cato on the past and the present.

C. I. STUDY ON THE PAGAN EMPIRE. — AUGUSTUS TO CONSTANTINE, 27 B.C.–323 A.D.

Discussion of Map-Questions. — The questions on p. 192 are so easy and general, that the teacher may introduce a pleasing variety by allowing their discussion to come up in a class-room conversation without any previous preparation.

Even from the first, the division of the Empire into a Latin half and a Greek and Oriental half was predestined. From Trieste eastward, the bulk of the towns were founded and inhabited by Greeks and Orientals, and were mistresses of lands and peoples stamped for centuries by Greek and Oriental culture. From Trieste westward, the towns were mostly of Roman foundation, and set in the midst of a barbarism untouched even in the days of Pericles. The only exceptions important to note are the southern parts of Spain and Italy, where the Greek and Oriental mixture always strongly modified the Latin element.

The two facts of the large number of cities in the Empire, and of their position, almost without exception, on the coast, or on river-courses, indicate the general commercial activity of the Empire; but "All roads led to Rome."

The studies on the Pagan Empire may be summarized somewhat as follows: —

PAGAN EMPIRE, 27 B.C. – 323 A.D.

Central Organization: Imperialism, tending to hereditary despotism.
    Centralized in
        person of emperor.
        city of Rome (*citizens of Rome* have the highest rights and privileges possible under the Empire).
    Supported by
        standing army, substantial basis of power.
        general taxation, severest in the provinces.[1]
        adulation and adoration (deification) of emperors.
        republican forms and titles.
    Dependent for excellence on
        character of emperors; *e.g.*, Nero and the Antonines.
    Bonds of union:
        Language, —
            Latin in West.
            Greek in East.[2]
        Law and government.
        Worship (adoration of emperor).[3]
        Easy communication by roads, seas, rivers.

Local Organizations: Municipal, republican, democratic, similar to the organization of republican Rome, which the cities of the West largely copied.

Tendencies and Characteristics.
    Growth of Greek and Oriental influence, seen in
        literature and art.
        language.
        religion (*Christianity*).

---

[1] Indeed, to use the telling phrase of Prof. Seeley, the provinces were "the great estates" of Rome, whose revenues fed and clothed her citizens.

[2] Note that the East roughly corresponds to the old Alexandrian Empire.

[3] Jews and Christians were monotheists, and so could not join the body of the Empire consistently in this regard; hence, one reason for their constant persecution.

PAGAN EMPIRE. — *Continued.*
    Practical bent of Roman mind, seen in
        native forms of literature, — history and contemporary criticism.
        public works, — baths, bridges, aqueducts, amphitheatres.
    Growth of Christianity, —
        seen in
            imperial persecutions.
            growth of Christian literature (compare third century with first).
            importance of heresies, threatening disunion.
        favored by
            unity and peace of Empire.
            decay of old religions.
    Progressive civilization and equalization of the provinces,[1] seen in
        origin and education of great men.
        universal suffrage given by Caracalla.
    Differentiation of East and West in
        language, —
            Latin (West).
            Greek (East).
        municipal foundations and populations.
        civilization, —
            Latin (West).
            Greek and Oriental (East).
        thought (note Eastern origin of heresies).
    Development of municipal centres of influence and culture.
        Rome.
        Alexandria.
        Antioch.
        Carthage.
    Comparative peace and order.
    Decline of third century seen in
        deterioration of literature and art.
        constant civil war.

---

[1] That Spain came first into prominence was probably due to her earlier conquest by Rome, and possibly to her still earlier contact with Phœnicians.

        growing difficulties with barbarians, indicated by
            new defences of Rome.
        frontier wars.
        development of hereditary despotism, —
            Diocletian.
        change and deterioration of population.[1]
Ideals:
        among the Pagans, — wealth, leisure, pleasure.
        among the Christians, — a pure, upright, brave, modest,
            industrious, self-denying, *Christlike* man.

Permanent Remains of Civilization.
    Literature, — history, poetry.
    Roads.
    Laws.
    The Christian religion.
    Languages, — French, Spanish, Italian.
    Cultivated lands of Latin countries.
    Architectural forms, — arch and dome.

The first question on p. 205 is intended to test the student's understanding of the word "constitutional," as applied to *organic* changes in government; such changes occurred in the transference of municipal elections from the assemblies to the Senate, under Tiberius; in the introduction of provincials to the Senate, under Claudius; in the new powers given by Hadrian to the Council of State; in the extension of citizenship to every freeman of the Empire by Caracalla. These changes were all in the line of a natural development of the imperial constitution, and culminated at last in that radical step taken by Diocletian, — the division of the Empire between despotic rulers of the Oriental type. It is worth noting that equality grew with despotism; or, to put it more justly, subjects ceased to rise, as rulers gained more universal power; and the provincial basis of the power of the emperor received new illustration from the fact that, in the process of equalization,

---

[1] As the Roman populations decay, barbarian elements are substituted for them, especially in the army.

the provincials gained. Indeed, the provincials were the chief gainers by the whole imperial system; no emperor would for a moment have tolerated such bad management as that of Verres and his fellows; to rule the province well for the emperor meant that it should be protected from invasion and disorder, that its internal resources should be fully developed, and that its people should, on the whole, be contented with their Roman master.

With the universal loss of actual freedom, with the growth of great armies under rival generals, and the increasing custom of deciding the imperial succession by civil war, it was perhaps well that the hereditary principle should gradually come to be recognized; for, while it subjected the Empire to the chance of birth, this was perhaps no worse a chance to run than that of the decision of war, while at least it relieved men from the confusion and anarchy of this latter method. Under either method, the great fault of the constitution was, that, resting as it did on a purely military basis, it neither represented nor developed, but, on the contrary, repressed the moral and intellectual strength of the Empire, and that, too, in the direction of government, where such forces were most sorely needed.

In the lists of great men and works in the imperial period we find simply the natural development of the practical Roman genius. We see that works on history, science, law, biography, far outweighed in number and general value the productions of the poet or philosopher. The one great original poet, Horace, was clever rather than great, and acquired popularity by the graceful ease with which he satirized the actual world; while Virgil appealed to the pride of the Roman race by singing in a half historic form their own ancestral glories.

In art the same tendency is to be noticed; whenever Rome broke away from the influence of Greek subjects, she at once left the company of gods and heroes, and sought to delineate, without idealizing, the famous men, the striking scenes and characters of contemporary life.

The study on p. 218 is intended rather to bring fresh proofs in support of previous points than to convey any new information. The extract from Virgil, p. 212, shows how easily an emperor like Augustus was regarded as a god, since, like the Roman deities in general, he procured for the people material blessings. The extract from Epictetus shows us, in a word, what these blessings were, and that, though the Romans had no longer either liberty or courage (see Tacitus), they had, at least, peace and order, and freedom of movement. This, in fact, was the sole glory of the Empire.

Even these material blessings were not unmixed; Tiberius felt it when he pointed out to the Senate (p. 213) the absolute dependence of Italy on the provinces for her daily food. But the great faults of the imperial period were, after all, moral; they are seen in that indifferent, selfish temper, which made "all Rome guilty of this Nero"; in that avarice and jealousy of the legions, in that flattery and cowardice of citizens and senators alike, to which Otho owed the purple; in that atmosphere whose interest centred in horses and gladiators; in that good-natured, fashionable contempt for labor, voiced by Pliny. All these influences were constantly educating a new generation into the typical Roman life of the period, while, according to Tacitus, they were strengthened rather than opposed by the educational surroundings of the child.

It is a grave question how far the individual was to blame for all this demoralization. A society organized on a slave basis, by virtue of that very fact cannot respect labor; and the centralization of power in the hands of one man always tends to weaken the minds and morals of those subjected to it, — two mighty causes of wide-spread evils.

At the close of all the discussions and summaries of this period, the teacher may, if he think best, thus summarize the contrasts between the Roman Empire and the Christian Church, considering both simply as historic organizations, brought into sharper and sharper contrast as the fourth century approached: —

	Roman Empire.	Christian Church.
Founded on	force of arms.	force of ideas and faith in them.
Bonds of union	government, law, language, formal worship of the emperor.	belief in the fatherhood of one God, and the brotherhood of all men.
Social distinctions	based on birth, wealth, and occupation.	none; equality of all classes and races before God, a predominant teaching.
Morality	based on selfishness.	based on unselfishness.
Ideals	the emperor, the wealthy man of leisure, the high official.	the Christlike man.

It will be noted in this contrast what mutually destructive agencies were arrayed against each other. Christianity entered the ancient world to maintain the manhood and brotherhood of the slave or the alien; to preach the existence of one God and of no other; to preach a morality based on love and self-denial. By virtue of these facts alone it attacked the whole framework of ancient society, which rested so firmly on bonds of kinship and a polytheistic worship, which had come to regard a standing army as the condition of life itself, and whose best morality was an enlightened selfishness. Since that framework was largely wrought in favor of privileged classes, we see at once why Christianity was so fiercely attacked by the empire and so fondly and rapidly embraced by "the Many."

Suggestions for Essay and Examination Work. — The debt of Rome to Alexander. The debt of France and Spain to Rome. Parallel between the Emperor Augustus and the Greek "tyrants." Suppose that Brutus and Cassius had won at Philippi, instead of Octavian, what then? A journey from Rome to London, 100 A.D. The Roman citizen the aristocrat of the Empire, 100 A.D. Journal of a Gallic soldier who was sent from the Rhine frontier to Memphis. Did the provinces conquer Rome, or Rome the provinces? The power behind the imperial throne. Reflections of a Christian in the

Colosseum, 90 A.D. When did the changes formally made by Diocletian begin in reality? Where did political liberty still exist at 300 A.D.? The foreign debt of Roman literature. The Roman road *v.* the Phœnician ship. What is the most universal bond of union you have yet found in your study of history?

STUDY ON THE TEUTONIC BARBARIANS.

The general results of the study may be tabulated as follows: —

THE TEUTONIC BARBARIANS.

Organization: Tribal — aristocratic and local.
    Units and bonds of union:
        patriarchic family, — kinship-bond.
        village community and mark-moot, — political unit with kinship-bond and bond of common property; supported by agriculture.
        warrior-band, — bonds of loyalty to a leader and a common interest; supported by booty of war.
    Classes of society and occupations (believed of divine origin):
        serfs, — hard manual labor.
        freemen, — artisans and directors.
        nobles, — warriors.
    Magistrates:
        kings or chiefs, chosen for birth; supported by gifts.
        chieftains, heads of warrior-bands; supported by plunder.
        judges, chosen by the people for ability.
    Assemblies:
        mark-moot, — general village assembly, purely local.
        assembly of chiefs, — deliberative.
        general assembly of freeborn warriors, — declares war, makes law, elects leaders and citizens, judges.

Characteristics.
    Bases of life:
        war, seen in vocabulary and songs, and in warrior-band.
        agriculture, seen in vocabulary and in village community.
    Independent, local, democratic tendency in politics.

The Teutonic Barbarians. — *Continued.*
    Love of independence.
    Insecurity of society.
    Strength and influence of women.
    Generous hospitality; scorn of manual (serf) labor.
    Ideal, — warrior.
Race-Relationship, Aryan: seen in organizations, vocabulary, myths, ideas.

Although this is a short study, it should be treated with marked care, since we now meet a fundamentally new type of society. Ancient Greece and Rome were "city-states,"[1] the powers of modern Europe are "country-states."[1] The history of the former began in an Acropolis or Capitol; that of the latter starts from the village and the canton; the city-state was an independent unit; the village and the canton are related by their organization to a larger area and population than their own. These differences developed greater, but at first the resemblances between the primitive groups of Teutons, Greeks, and Romans were more pronounced than their differences. Even that fundamental fact in the Teutonic village, the common possession of land apportioned by the majority votes of the marks-men, seems to be matched by the division of public lands among the Roman citizens; although, in the former case, the matter was far more closely connected with the very foundation of the state, and the land was not only divided, but managed by the mark-moot. But positive and unquestioned resemblances are to be found in the assemblies. Thus the Teutonic assembly of chiefs matched the Homeric assembly of Elders, the Areopagus, the various senates; to the mark-moot corresponded the Agora, the Ekklesia, the Centuries, and the Tribes; everywhere appeared the kinship-bond and the patriarchal family. Between magistrates it is more difficult to draw the parallel, since the god-born king among the Teutons seems at first subordinate to the warlike chief whom a tribe may

---

[1] These terms are borrowed from Prof. J. R. Seeley.

choose to follow. This determination of rank by might in war finds illustration again in the fact that admission to the full political and military status of a Teuton was only won by proved ability in arms, although Teutonic birth gave the first right to the Teutonic name; and the kinship-bond had been so purely preserved, that, to Tacitus, the people appeared of pure, unmingled race. Once admitted to full Teutonic privileges, however, the individual found himself a free and equal member of a democratic community.

Throughout this work the teacher should keep it well before the mind of the pupil that, in a more special sense than before, he is studying the origin of his own people and kin-folk, of his own ancestors in direct lineage. The following little table will show him how we stand in the great Aryan relationship: —

EUROPEAN ARYAN STOCK.

Keltic: Irish, Scotch, Welsh.
Teutonic: Germans, English, Scandinavians, Americans.
Slavic: Russians, Servians, and other Christian peoples of the Balkan peninsula, to a greater or less degree.
Græco-Italian: The Greeks and Romans of antiquity.

Since the directions and dates of the early Aryan migrations are still in the field of theory, it is best for the teacher, while allowing surmise, to discourage positive statements. That the migrations must have antedated 1000 B.C. is sure enough, from the fact of the then-established Greek, Italian, and Keltic peoples, fully separated by speech and habits. Geographical distribution, again, points with apparent clearness to a general movement from the region of the Black Sea, although the question of the original home of the Aryans is by no means settled. For a complete and recent discussion of the whole Aryan question, see Dr. O. Schrader's "Prehistoric Antiquities of the Aryan Peoples." Translated by Jevons, London, 1890. We have some evidence in the common vocabulary of the house and field for maintaining that, before their separation, the Aryans already had in common possession the arts of agriculture, and some primitive form of navigation; that their flocks supplied the wool they wove and wore, while their herds performed for them the labors of the field, and furnished them the products of the dairy, which, with ground grain, made the staples of their food.

Suggestions for Essay and Examination Work. — A visit to the primitive Aryans before their separation into the various European races. The mark-moot and the New England town meeting. Compare the Teutonic ideal of womanhood with our own. Reflections of a Teutonic prisoner of Julius Cæsar on what he saw at Rome. The Aryan bonds of union.

C. II. THE CHRISTIAN EMPIRE. — CONSTANTINE TO CHARLEMAGNE.

This division of the imperial history at the name and date of Constantine is popular rather than accurate; although, as the founder of Constantinople, he appeared to the popular mind as the founder of the Eastern Empire, yet Diocletian had in reality been the first thus to divide the Roman dominion. Led to victory and converted, as he maintained, by the sign of the cross, and the first of the emperors to give Christianity high rank in the faiths of the Empire, Constantine has naturally been considered the founder of its temporal power, although it did not become the legal faith of Rome until the days of Theodosius. But since great and stirring events and influential myths have gathered about the name of Constantine, and since the great changes attributed to him did in reality receive from him their greatest impetus, it has seemed best for the purposes of a popular text-book to take advantage of the popular tendency to link the great events of an age with its greatest name.

After 476 no more attention is paid to the Eastern Empire than is necessary in order thoroughly to understand the general history of Europe; for, from that time, it follows its inevitable tendency to become an Oriental state, tempered and colored by the Greek culture.

II. A. THE CHRISTIAN EMPIRE UNDER ROMAN CONTROL.

The studies on pp. 231–250, inclusive, may be summarized as follows:—

CHRISTIAN EMPIRE.—CONSTANTINE TO ODOVAKER AND THEODORIC.

Organization of State: Oriental despotism.
    Centred
        at Rome and Constantinople.
        in persons of the emperors.
    Supported by
        forced taxes.
        barbarian armies.
        favor of privileged, powerful classes,—
            officials.
            soldiers.
            clergy.

Organization of Church: Parallel to, and united with that of the state.
    Centred
        at Rome and Constantinople.
        in hands of bishops and emperors.
    Based on and supported by
        the belief and trust of men.
        conversion of barbarian masses.
            Goths.
            Visigoths.
            Irish.
        imperial edicts [1] (suppression of Paganism).
        favor of the poor, oppressed, neglected *majority*.

---

[1] As *Pontifex Maximus*, the emperor was naturally regarded as the legal and temporal head of the church,

CHRISTIAN EMPIRE. — *Continued.*
    Marked by
        internal unity, resulting from
            suppression of heresy.
            orthodox standard of faith, —
                Council of Nice, 325 A.D.
        acquirement by bishops of
            privilege.
            wealth.
            judicial power.
        spirit and forms of democracy.

Characteristics of Period:
    Growth of Teutonic power
        caused by
            constitution of armies, composed of and officered by barbarians.
            settlement of Teutons as laborers, and owners of imperial soil in Gaul, Italy, Spain, and the lands of the Danube.
        culminating in so-called "Fall of Western Empire."
        shaped by Roman influence in
            religious organization and faith.
            military and political organization.
            ideals (see speech of Adolphus, p. 249).
    Pervading influence and power of Christianity,
        seen in
            organization.
            persecution of Paganism.
            law.
            predominant taste for religious literature.
            Arian controversy.[1]

---

[1] The intensity with which men were interested in theology is best seen in that large fact of the irreconcilable hostility of the Arian barbarian and the orthodox provincial. That this hostility was primarily religious is proved by the fact that in Gaul, during the next period, the orthodox barbarian Franks easily mingled with the orthodox provincials. This violent hostility thoroughly justified to the men of that time the attempts of emperors and councils to enforce that unity of belief which meant both peace and power. Compare with the feeling often roused in modern times between Protestants and Catholics.

the new saint-ideal, resulting in *monastic organization*.
new materials (biblical and religious), in art and literature.[1]
mingled with pagan and heathen ideas.
employed to
    humanize law.
    modify absolutism (Theodosius and Ambrose).
    protect the poor and oppressed.

Intellectual leadership of East,
seen in
    predominating proportion of literary centres, — Alexandria, Athens. Antioch, Cæsarea.
    origin of literary men.
    origin of monastic ideal and of heresies.

Moral decay of Rome,
seen in
    imperial absolutism (see laws).
    corruption (bribery) and extravagance of courts; ∴
    corruption and extravagance of fashionable life.
    servility, superstition, idleness.
    gluttony and luxury.
resulting in
    hatred of Rome by her own subjects.
    oppression of over-taxed provinces.

All the facts of this obscure but most important period clustered about three centres, — the church, the Empire, and the barbarians. These three centres were, however, connected in vital relations. The church and the barbarians took to themselves all that was yet alive and of worth in the decaying Empire. Her intellectual and moral energy passed to the church; her military and political power to the barbarians;

---

[1] Although in its beginnings Christian art could claim neither beauty nor truth, it was nevertheless original in its materials and impulses. In this originality lay the promise of the new development and inspiration which was to culminate in Raphael and Michael Angelo.

this receives fine illustration from the fact that in the fourth and fifth centuries of her history, the great names were either those of bishops and popes, or those of war-chiefs and generals. The bishops and popes belonged to the civilized provincials, while the generals and war-chiefs were pure barbarian leaders.[1] This one fact shows how the force of the Empire, leaving its old forms, deadened by despotism, and its old populations, spoiled and helpless through luxury and moral decay, was urging its way into fresh forms and among new peoples.

So long as the Empire had appeared to rule for the greatest benefit of the greatest number, the sting of despotism was concealed; but in the fifth century it was, in the sight of all men, an organization managed in behalf of the ease, wealth, power, and pleasure of the emperor and his officials. In this regard, it was a striking contrast to the Athens of Pericles, or to Punic Rome, where the state was organized in behalf of the whole body of citizens. This contrast was still further heightened by the fact that it was precisely on the whole body of citizens that the burdens of government fell; the " curiales," the " decurions," the free, but untitled citizens of Rome were just those whom she deprived of arms for self-defense, and from whom she extorted the taxes demanded to support the pomp and waste of four courts, and the establishments of countless officials, to say nothing of the justifiable charges of a government defending an enormous frontier by professional troops.

When the imperial government became so thoroughly a matter of routine, its excellence still depended partly on the personal character of the emperor, but more on his power to select men fit to serve him as generals, secretaries, judges, since by these subordinates the business of the Empire was chiefly done.

---

[1] Yet it is interesting to note, that on the military greatness of the barbarian, Rome depended for her strength; while the intellectual and moral superiority of the Roman bishops was to spread civilization through the wider barbarian world.

So long as her soldiers remained true and obedient, and her lands productive, the Empire could hardly perish; since, with money and troops, with the favor of the bishops who led opinion and of the officials who executed law, it possessed essential strength. But as her soldiery was drawn more and more from barbarian peoples, and so became less and less in sympathy with the habits and ideas of the Empire, and as, by slave-culture, absentee landlords, and a constantly increasing tax-pressure, the utility of her lands was gradually destroyed, the change of 476 was inevitable.

The teacher must not allow the popular ideas of the "Fall of the Roman Empire" to influence him too strongly in his views of this change, which was in its reality a change in the proportions of population, and a shifting of power rather than a conquest. As soldiers and as laborers, the barbarians had long been entering the Empire, until, at 476, they composed the better and stronger part of her fighting and working people. For, as the love of leisure and pleasure had rendered the arduous labors of the camp distasteful to the Romans, these had fallen naturally to great warrior bands, who gladly entered a service so congenial to their love of warfare. So soon, however, as the strength of conscious organization was felt by armies practically barbarian, they naturally demanded recognized place and power in the Roman territory and among Roman officials, nor was there any force to withstand them. Although, in reality, political as well as military power had now passed into the hands of the Teutons, and the leadership of Western Europe was acknowledged to be theirs, still to a contemporary Roman this change could not have seemed so profound or startling as we now know it to have been; he would have stated the superficial apparent fact that through the weakness of the western government and the influence of the soldiery of Odovaker, both parts of the Empire were again united under the eastern emperor, who had now commissioned barbarian generals not only with the command of the legions, but also with the political management of the western provinces. By the provincials, indeed, such a change could not have been greatly deplored, since the Empire had become their oppressor rather than protector, and since, according to Salvian, at least (p. 248), many of them had already expressed their preference for barbarian rule.

In all this, Rome but reaped as she had sown. The new ideals of life and morals, which entered Rome in the first century B.C., naturally culminated in such a picture as that drawn by Ammianus (p. 244), and in the transfer of her power to the monk and the barbarian; in other words, to men whose ideal was the self-denying saint, or the warrior who could die on the hard-fought field.

Nevertheless, Rome had so long mastered the civilized world with law and the barbarian hordes with fear, that even in the midst of the weak confusion of the fifth century she seemed to the church the earthly prototype of the "City of God," while barbarian ambition looked to her as the shining centre of the world, the proudest source whence it could win its titles of command. This *name* that had gathered to itself for more than a thousand years all that the world contained of strength and beauty and order, did not easily lose its deeply rooted power; a power that must be reckoned with at least to the days of Charlemagne.

In considering the organization of the church, two fundamental facts must constantly be remembered; one is, that Christianity became the state faith of the Empire, the historical successor of Paganism.[1] The old temples were turned into churches; state privileges and revenues passed from the old orders of priests to the new; the whole organized framework of the Empire, with its central powers at Rome or Constanti-

---

[1] The extract given from the "City of God," p. 246, gives a curious illustration of the fact that, to the men of the fourth century, not only had one church and belief displaced another, but that actual supernatural powers, strong to work mischief to men, — deified evil spirits, in fact, — had been overthrown by the one true, beneficent God. Men no longer worshipped these old gods, but they still believed in them and feared them as devils and demons.

nople, with its municipalities acting as mediators between the provinces and the emperor, with its imperial Pontifex Maximus, with its network of roads and posts, became the framework of the church; from this point of view, the church appeared like a centralized hierarchy. But this other fact must always be remembered, that the strong officials of the church, the bishops, owed their power to popular elections, so that the government of the church might be described as a democracy, acting through a strongly organized centralization.

That Rome should become a more strongly pronounced centre than Constantinople is not surprising when we notice that Rome had not a single powerful, long-established city in the west as her rival, unless we except Carthage, while Constantinople was the child of yesterday to Antioch, Alexandria, or Damascus. Again, the power of the emperors after Constantine more decidedly centred at the eastern than the western capital; hence the power of the Roman bishop, left untrammeled by the imperial presence, grew more freely and strongly than that of the bishop of Constantinople; and again, the name of Rome carried with it through all the West a power of mighty and ancient tradition, in which the "New Rome," Constantinople, was entirely wanting.

Suggestions for Essay and Examination Work. — Complaint of a decurion. The power of the church at 476 A.D. compared with that of the Empire. Constantine and Julian. The political value of a fixed creed. Famous barbarians of the later empire. What had the barbarian to give to the Empire? Journal of a Roman Christian, ransomed by St. Ambrose from the Germans beyond the Rhine. St. Anthony. What resemblances between the saint-ideal of the fourth and fifth centuries and the warrior-ideal? The conquests of the church. Private reflections of Claudian on his patron Stilicho. Compare life at Rome, in the days of Ammianus, with that in the days of Cincinnatus.

II. *B and C.* THE WEST UNDER BARBARIAN CONTROL; EMPIRE OF CHARLEMAGNE.

Summarize the studies, pp. 250–285, somewhat as follows : —

CHRISTIAN EMPIRE, 476–814. — ODOVAKER – CHARLEMAGNE.

Organization of State, 476–800 A.D.
    In East: Oriental despotism, centred at Constantinople.
    In West: Delegation or abandonment of imperial power to bishops of Rome.
        barbarian kings and generals in Spain, France, Italy, Britain, Africa.[1]

Organization of State under Charlemagne.
    Restoration of name and style of Western emperors.
    Union of spiritual and temporal powers of pope and emperor in "Holy Roman Empire."[2]

Organization of Church.
    Development of centralized papal power.
    Development of monasticism (*Benedictine order*).

Characteristics of Period in the Empire.
    Growing separation of East and West.[3]

---

[1] Although this power was a delegated one, the barbarian leaders, as generals of well-disciplined forces, held the actual military power of Europe; while, as titled officers of the Empire, they gained the traditional power of its *name;* add to this that they were generally the chosen or hereditary native commanders of their armies.

[2] The mosaic of St. John, in Lateran (p. 275), shows pictorially the fundamental ideas that underlay this Holy Roman Empire. By their size and relative position pope and emperor appear as equals, inferior to their Lord Christ, from whom they take their different powers as his delegates on earth. The account of the "Crowning of Charlemagne" again (p. 274), clearly shows that to himself and the men of his day Charlemagne was the "anointed of the Lord," and the source of his power divine, like that of the warrior-kings of Israel.

[3] After the Mohammedan conquests we find Islam dividing, like the Roman Empire, into an eastern and a western part. Is it not possible that the old differences thus made themselves once more felt?

THE WEST UNDER BARBARIAN CONTROL.

> Favored by
>> difference in language [1] and culture.
>> inability of East to hold and govern the West; ∴.
>> imperial abandonment of Rome to ecclesiastic and barbarian control.
>
> Culminating in
>> crowning of Charlemagne by pope, 800.
>
> Predominance of ecclesiastical power in the West.
>> Caused or favored by
>>> imperial weakness and neglect.
>>> conversion of barbarians [2] ("*conquests of Christian Empire*"),—
>>>> Goths.
>>>> Vandals.
>>>> Irish.
>>>> Franks.
>>>> Burgundians.
>>>> Saxons in England.
>>>> Saxons in Germany (Charlemagne).
>>>> Scotch.
>>>
>>> protective attitude of church toward poor and oppressed.
>>> monopoly of Roman civilization, centred in *monasteries*.
>>
>> Resulting or appearing in
>>> temporal power of popes and bishops,—
>>>> political.
>>>> military.
>>>> legal and judicial.

---

[1] Although modern languages began to assert themselves, still Latin was the tongue of the thinking and governing classes and the language of literature.

[2] It is not generally sufficiently insisted upon that while the "barbarians" overran the Empire, Christianity almost at once permeated the barbarians, thus subjecting the strongest peoples of Europe to the religious organization and faith of the later Empire; this subjection was aided by the impression which the Roman Empire and the Roman church still made upon the barbarians through its splendor, wealth, and titles (see p. 273, Conversion of Clovis).

CHRISTIAN EMPIRE. — *Continued.*
>> development of asceticism, embodied in monastic organization, —
>>> idealizing self-denial and benevolence.
>>> opposing violence and selfishness.
>>> encouraging labor and learning.
>> union of West in
>>> faith.
>>> language.
>>> law.
>>> ideals (monastic, saintly).
>> religious character of intellectual interests.
>> civilizing influences (largely monastic) in direction of
>>> literature (chiefly monkish history and literature).
>>> music.[1]
>>> law (humanizing it).
>>> industrial and decorative arts, science.
>>> morality and humanity.
>>> agriculture.
> Hindered by
>> mixture and corruption of Christianity by
>>> paganism (demonology), and heresy.
>>> misunderstanding of its teachings (*Clovis*).
> Culminating in establishment of
> "HOLY ROMAN EMPIRE."

Romanizing of the Teuton in
> religion — Christianity.
> language and literature.
> law.
> military tactics.
> agriculture and industry (monasteries).

Provincial confusion and misery.
> Caused by
>> weak government.
>> barbarian attack, invasion, and change.

---

[1] It will be noted that music, painting and the arts of decoration owe their modern impulse to the mediæval church.

THE WEST UNDER BARBARIAN CONTROL. 79

  Saracenic invasion.
  prevalence of personal rather than territorial law.[1]
 Resulting in
  weakness of art and literature.
  corruption of Latin (begins to change to French, Italian, Spanish).
  strengthening of Teutonic provincial governments.
Growth of vital power in West, seen in
  production of great men (bishops and warriors).
  military and political vigor of the Teuton,[2] culminating in Charlemagne.
  appearance of Western tongues in literature,—
   English ⎫
   French ⎬ indicating
   Irish   ⎭
  intellectual advance of peoples.
  attempts at legal order.
Rapid growth of Mohammedan faith and empire.
 Caused or favored by
  simplicity of belief.
  heretical disaffection of Egypt and Syria toward Constantinople.[3]
 Resulting in
  imperial loss of
   Syria, — Damascus, Antioch.
   Egypt, — Memphis (Cairo), Thebes.
   Africa. Carthage.
 Checked by Spain.
  orthodox defenders, —
   Leo at Constantinople.
   Charles Martel at Tours.

---

[1] According to *personal* law, a man is judged by the law of his own people, wherever he may be; according to *territorial* law, he is judged by the law of the land in which he dwells, no matter whence he came.

[2] This vigor had a double source, — the unbroken, warlike tastes of the Teuton and his heritage of Roman military tactics.

[3] Compare the cases of Africa and Spain, which had been or were still under the power of *Arians*, who could easily accept the bare monotheism of Mohammed.

The points made from study to study in regard to Mohammedanism had better be tabulated, as far as possible, by themselves, in order to preserve unity of view. The following is offered as suggestive : —

THE SARACENS.

Conquests, Religious.

Government, Despotic Theocracy (Omar, Haroun; see relation of palace and mosque, p. 281).

Religious Doctrines.
    Monotheism.
    Divine inspiration
        of prophets, — Moses, Christ, *Mohammed.*
        of Koran, — revealed to Mohammed.
    Fore-ordained necessity of all events (fatalism).[1]
    Immortality of the soul.
    Future rewards and punishments (of material sort).[1]

Religious Duties.
    Prayer, fasting.
    Alms-giving, pilgrimage.
    Moral life according to Moslem standards, which
        allows polygamy, ∴
        produces subjection of women, modified by
            natural and religious feeling.
        condemns drunkenness and gaming.
        condemns cruelty to animals.
        preaches charity,[2] faithfulness, justice, resignation.

Civilization, at first simple, pastoral, and religious (*Omar*), becomes highly artistic, scientific, and material (*Haroun-al-Raschid*).
    Centering at[3]

Bagdad.	Cairo.
Damascus.	Cordova.

---

[1] To these doctrines are generally ascribed a good part of the fighting energy of the Saracenic forces.

[2] The practical effect of this morality may be seen in the moderate treatment of Eastern Christians (see pp. 279, 280).

[3] Note also the Mohammedan possession of Antioch and Alexandria, and of Assyria, Egypt, and Persia, with their old civilized centres.

Developing
- Moorish architecture and ornament, —
    - horseshoe arch, *dome* (compare St. Sophia).
    - minaret (spire), arabesque.[1]
    - trefoil and quatrefoil.
- scientific study of
    - mathematics.[2]
    - astronomy.[2]
    - medicine.[2]
    - philosophy (Aristotle).
- commercial intercourse of East and West.
- industrial and agricultural activity; weaving, embroidery, metal-work, pottery, dyeing, inlaid work in wood and marble, horticulture, leather work (Morocco), manufacture of figured silk (damask).

Springing from
- Greek and Oriental sources.

Two things beyond all others marked this age. The first was the pervading and progressive power of religion; in the West, the church predominated as a political and legal as well as an intellectual and moral influence; in the East, political differences were confirmed by heresies, until at last all were alike swept away by the irresistible tide of Mohammedanism and its simple monotheistic faith. The second thing was the mixture of influences produced by the constant mixture of peoples; the church gave to the barbarian the civilization as well as the faith of Rome, and her monks, travelling as missionaries or envoys, from end to end of Europe, did much to create

---

[1] The beauty of the arabesque, and of Moorish work in general, depends not only on the skilful and intricate mingling of symmetrical mathematical forms, but also upon delicate and brilliant combinations of color; the former quality pleasing the mind, and the latter the sense. The strict observance of the second commandment having prevented any development of sculpture or figure painting, the whole artistic talent of the Moors was turned to the lesser arts of pure *decoration*, in which, perhaps, they have never been excelled.

[2] Compare the Alexandrian civilization.

a united Christendom; of these monks, there is no better type than Theodore of Tarsus, a Greek, sent by the Roman bishop to found the English Canterbury (p. 262). While the church penetrated the wilderness, the peoples of the wilderness constantly penetrated the Empire; invasion, settlement, conversion, mingled old and new, culture and barbarism, good and evil; the church alone being fixed, little by little mastered the confusion. Perhaps no one thing better showed the varied influences of the time than Western law, which based itself alike on the written codes of Rome and on Teutonic custom, while both were modified by the ever-present advice and aid of the bishops.

In the East, on the other hand, Islam was the mingling power, which carried rude pastoral tribes into ancient and highly civilized lands, whose finest culture they made their own, though " with a difference," and whence they conveyed it to the farthest West, which was still inferior to the East in all material and artistic ways.[1]

In the West, the crowning of Charlemagne was the culmination of the growing separation of the East and the West, of the developing temporal power of the Western church, and of the actual Teutonic as opposed to the nominal imperial rule; for although the name of Roman emperor was heard again in the West, still the "Holy Roman Empire" embodied a revolt, and Charlemagne's title was usurped; the new Empire covered new territories unknown to Roman rule, embraced the heart of modern Europe with the Rhine valley for its centre, comprised new populations and tongues, held its power as the temporal arm of the church, and as a gift from its spiritual head. In

---

[1] Historians often contend that the Moors had no original civilization, since they took their architectural and decorative "motives" from Constantinople, Damascus, or Persia, their science from Alexandria and Syria, their philosophy from Aristotle. Without insisting on a decision, it may be noted that they so advanced or modified or mingled what they took, that they left upon it such a distinctive mark of *character* as to demand a separate name for what is Moorish or Arabian.

spite of these fundamental differences, the tradition of Rome was still so strong as to force her name on any ruler who could pretend to hold the West together ; hence the value of receiving the imperial title from the Bishop of Rome, the only man left in Europe, except the Eastern emperor, who could be said to represent in historic line the authority of the ancient Empire ; thus received, too, the imperial title gained the sanction of religion, and the Empire could, as "Holy," claim the alliance of all Christendom ; from this time on, the names of Roman and Christian were synonymous in the West, and from this point of view we see the necessity which Charlemagne felt of converting the Saxons before incorporating them into his empire.

Although artistic, poetic, or pure intellectual genius was rare in this period, the fact was probably due to the circumstances of obscurity and confusion, which marked the time, since of greatness there was no lack, but it was a greatness that displayed itself in action, feeling, and character rather than in vision. Nevertheless, I have chosen the motto on p. 228, because, in spite of the clang and movement of the age, its real strength lay in quiet, germinal, partly unconscious powers, moving like leaven amid the troubled mass.

Suggestions for Essay and Examination Work. — "And after the fire, a still small voice." Clovis, patrician of Rome. What causes made the way of the Mohammedan conquests into the Empire comparatively easy? The strength of the pope. The visit of St. Augustine to Britain. Comparison of Augustus, emperor, with Charlemagne, emperor. Was the so-called "conversion" of the Saxons justifiable? (Debate.) Why should Pope Gregory be called "Great"? Reasons why a Goth became a Benedictine monk. Visit to Monte Cassino. Why should Justinian be the most famous emperor of this period? The Mohammedan bonds of union. The character of Omar. Journey of Theodore of Tarsus to England. The court of Charlemagne. Why should Charlemagne become the hero of western Europe? Compare Omar and Haroun-al-Raschid.

EUROPEAN HISTORY, 814–1880.

INTRODUCTORY.

Before the ninth century, the centre of political interest lay at Rome or Constantinople; but with the death of Charlemagne, the power of Rome began to fade, political interest began to gather about various national centres and national heroes, and the modern states of Europe began to appear in undefined and nascent forms. Within two centuries, France, England, Germany, Spain, and Italy were known and feared as powers. From that time on, the history of Europe has presented a complex, continuous development along original lines, though starting from those of antiquity. For this reason, the history of more than a thousand years is massed under the single title of European as opposed to Greek and Roman history.

From the beginning through, the teacher should have well in mind the great trends and marks of the long and complex period. First, then, we have to do with *constantly enlarging political areas*. Cities are no longer the political units of history, but countries,[1] and countries that grow first to their full natural boundaries in Europe, and then begin to possess and assimilate the lands of America, Asia, and Africa. Cities still exist, not as rulers, but as condensed centres of the population and labor of their various countries.

Not only are the units larger, but they differ in their origin. In antiquity, the tribe, bound together by the tradition or reality of a common descent, was the original unit, which grew by successive adoptions of aliens. *A group of related men* formed the historic kernel of the state. From 800 on, *a parcel of land possessing common interests* forms this historic kernel, and

---

[1] For this distinction I am indebted to Prof. J. R. Seeley.

gradually draws its inhabitants together into the *nation-unit*, which holds men together by attachment to a common fatherland, as of old they were held together by attachment to a common ancestor.

A third point to be noted is *the development of this unit*. This parcel of land, held at first by many nobles, under the nominal lead of a king, is, during the mediæval period, the cause of long and hard contention between its rival claimants. In the age of the Renaissance, this contention culminates in the formation of strong, centralized monarchies in France, England, and Spain; while in Germany and Italy, a multitude of strong cities and rival princes rise, weakening their country in behalf of their separate individualities. In the modern period, both phases have given place in various ways to strong, united nations, tending more and more to popular constitutions, with a growing tendency to make the state the agent of all common service, in government, education, transportation, and even in more radical ways.

The fourth and last point to be held in mind is that, along with this development of individual nations, has gone *the development of a European commonwealth*. By the constantly increasing complex of international relations, weaving together inextricably the interests of neighboring states, a Christianized, European, Aryan unit has been formed as against less civilized continents, held by other faiths and peoples.

These four points all relate to the political development of Europe; I have not thought it necessary to call special attention to the other marked tendencies of the whole period, such as the growth of knowledge and free thought, the development of a popular material civilization, the acquisition of freedom in various forms; for while these movements are of the highest importance, they are easy to see and simple to understand.

A. EARLY MEDIÆVAL PERIOD. — CHARLEMAGNE TO THE CRUSADES, 814–1095.

The studies from p. 291 to p. 318 inclusive may be summarized as follows: —

THE CIVILIZED WORLD, 814–1095.

Organizations of Period.
    Feudal units (fiefs), —
        bound together by
            loyalty.
            interest.
            possession of and residence on common land.
        forming weak monarchies in
            France.
            England.
            Spain.
            Italy and Germany.
    Holy Roman Empire, —
        temporal, imperial powers embodied in emperor.
        spiritual, sacerdotal powers embodied in pope.
    Oriental despotisms in
        Byzantine Empire.
        caliphates.

Characteristics of Period.
    In feudal monarchies.
        Land, basis of power, seen in
            change of law from personal to territorial.
            service of the inferior dependent on land-grants from the superior.
            theory that king is the land-owner of kingdom.
            government co-extensive with estates.
        Growth of landed aristocracy,[1] with strong class-distinctions (great inequality).

---

[1] Curiously enough, this aristocracy has survived in its purest feudal form in England, where it was at first constitutionally most subject to the king (from 1066 onward).

Decentralization of power,
> seen in
>> wars of feudal lords against kings.
>> control of kings by feudal lords.
>> numerous feudal units.
> resulting in
>> constant petty warfare ("Truce of God").
> Partial, arbitrary, and conflicting law.[1]
> Insecurity of trade.
> Loss of individual liberty.

In Holy Roman Empire.
> Weakness of imperialism (*no land*).
> Power based on religious faith (see imperial style and title).
> Centralization of power in hands of pope, culminating in *Hildebrand*.
> Closer definition of German frontier, caused by invasion and threatened invasion.

In Islam.
> Development of extravagant Oriental courts and monarchies.
> Growth of a scientific, material civilization, based on Oriental and Greek culture.
> Formation of new Mohammedan powers, —
>> Turkey in Asia.
>> Egypt.

In England.
> Royal power strengthened by
>> constant foreign invasion, uniting king and barons and people into a nation.
>> "immediate" oaths demanded by William the Conqueror.[2]
> Growth of English independence of continent seen in literature (*English*).

---

[1] Hence it often happened that in order to gain justice from a powerful baron, it was absolutely necessary to employ force against him, since there was no executive strong enough to compel men to obey any general law, even were such a law in existence.

[2] Before the time of William the Conqueror, the thanes seem to have had more constitutional power of interfering with general politics than the French barons. This power they seem to have retained while the "immediate" oaths demanded by William deprived them of absolute independence,

The Civilized World, 814–1095. — *Continued.*
In general.
Great confusion
arising from
barbarian invasions and attacks from Northmen in
Sicily, Italy.
France, England.
Turks and Hungarians in
Holy Roman Empire.
Byzantine Empire.
Islam.
feudalism.
causing
insecurity of trade.
insecurity of travel (pilgrims).
little intellectual and artistic life.
mixture of barbarism and civilization.
Formation of new states and powers, —
Hungary, Normandy, Austria,[1] Prussia,[1] Kingdom of Two Sicilies, in Europe.
Turkey[2] in Asia.
General mixture of European blood, —
in France: Roman, Kelt,[3] Frank, Norman.
in England: Kelt, Saxon, Norman.
in Italy: Roman, Kelt, Greek, Lombard, Norman, Arab.
in Spain: Kelt, Roman, Goth, Arab.

---

[1] I have asked what would account for the long succession of strong rulers in these two states; may not the answer be found in the fact that the founders of the Houses of Austria and Brandenburg were necessarily the picked men of their whole generation for vigorous physique and positive character?

[2] Compare the entrance of the Turks into Islam with that of the Teutons into the Empire. In both cases the conquerors were, in turn, subdued by the faith and culture of their subjects.

[3] It should here be noted that previous to the Roman conquests the Kelts were the leading people in France, Spain, and England, while they had a strong hold on the best part of Italy.

EARLY MEDIÆVAL PERIOD.

Complete separation of East and West,[1] —
    in government: "*Holy Roman Empire.*"
    in religion: "*Schism of the Church.*"
Traces of Greek influence in West, seen in
    literature (John Scotus).
    architecture (St. Mark's).
The church strongest power in Europe, —
    because of
        unity of government (strong papacy).
        unity of language (Latin).
        unity of faith (new barbarian kingdoms, Christian).
        possession of civilization, —
            literature, art.
            law, industries.
        hold on the minds of men through fear of excommunication, ∴
            eternal damnation.
        democratic spirit and organization
    seen in
        relation to temporal powers (see titles of emperor and kings).
        assumption of military and governmental powers (see "Truce of God" and call to the crusades).
        prevalent impulse to pilgrimage.
Traces of secularization, seen in
    tendencies of clergy to worldly pleasures and occupations.
    secular developments in literature, history, poetry, philosophy, etc.
    influence in temporal affairs.

---

[1] This separation was inevitable from the first; differences in language, culture, thought, style, had long been preparing the way for differences in faith and worship; and when at last this difference became pronounced, and the "Holy Roman Empire" an established fact, no bond of union any longer existed between the parts of the Empire, and they broke apart as naturally as the ripe fruit falls. No effort on the part of pope or emperor or patriarch could any longer sustain even the name of union.

THE CIVILIZED WORLD, 814–1095. — *Continued.*
    Tendency to revolt against the church, —
        in government (Investiture quarrels).
        in thought (John Scotus).[1]
    Spirit of church, —
        humane.
        democratic (offices open to all classes; see Hildebrand).
        intolerant of heresy (requiring unity).
        reformatory,[2] —
            restoration of asceticism.
            celibacy of clergy required.

The teacher cannot be too careful to have his pupils thoroughly understand the feudal organization, since it is the great secular foundation of European society and politics from the days of Charlemagne onward, and only began to lose its hold in the latter part of the seventeenth century. Its central fact was this, the *union of political, military, and legal power with the ownership of land;* the land-owner was the land-*lord.* In theory, the king was landlord over all. In need of men and money, he delegated his lands, and with them his powers to subordinate holders, who paid again by the use of land for service of body and purse. The possession of land was the measure of military and financial power; at once, then, we see the cause of the weakness of the early mediæval king as against a combination of two or three strong barons; we understand how the emperor,

---

[1] Although both Anselm and Scotus both wished to found theology on sound reason, yet when the two were in conflict, Anselm taught that reason should yield to authority, while the bolder spirit of Scotus announced that authority itself was "derived from reason." The letter from the pope concerning Erigena (p. 313) is interesting, as showing how thoroughly the former felt responsible for the purity of the faith, and therefore claimed the right to regulate European thought.

[2] Of course this spirit was only felt by the strongest and best, and culminated in Hildebrand, whose measures were the logical outcome of his desire to save the church from the cares and burdens and pleasures of the world, in order that it might more effectually rule and help the world,

gaining his title as a successor of the old Roman emperors, whose power was supported by taxation, found himself in possession of the name of ruler alone; for the feudal theory expected a sovereign "to live from his own," namely, lead his own vassals to war, and gain support from his own domains. The emperor, then, as emperor, had only such recognition as the temper and belief of the period might accord. From this point of view, we understand how important the question of investiture was to Henry IV., and how the emperor could only preserve imperial power in those countries where he was also king, in Germany and Italy, while France was practically lost to the Empire when she became an independent kingdom.

As for the effects of feudalism on liberty, equality, peace, and unity, he who runs may read; the effect on manners is more questionable. Guizot, in his History of Civilization, considers it good; but Ordericus Vitalis hardly encourages such an opinion for this age; during this period it is not safe, perhaps, to say much more than that class distinctions produce class manners, and that in a society of superiors and inferiors, formalities will necessarily arise, with tendencies to condescension on one side and servility on the other.

I have not called special attention in my Students' Edition to the resemblances between the Teutonic warrior band and the feudal unit; the feudal lord is the chosen chief, his superior vassals are his bravest companions, who still are bound together by a common loyalty and a still stronger common interest, but whom he now rewards, not, as in Cæsar's day, with spear and steed, but with permanent titles to land. In the feudal courts, again, we see the mark-moot, but with the all-important modification, that the war-leader has become a political and legal ruler, and thus destroys the village democracy; while in the feudal code of justice we find each man still his own defender and avenger. The teacher, however, must act his own judgment as to how far he should discuss the origin of feudalism, since the facts on which any theory can be built are fragmentary.

The extract given from Byrhtnoth's Death (p. 310) illustrates primitive feudalism perhaps at its best. Here we see England invaded by a Danish warrior band, evidently attracted thither by the comparative wealth of the land, now long settled by an agricultural people. Against them is arrayed the feudal unit,[1] led by Byrthnoth, who adds to sure confidence in the Christian faith, an English courage and determination to protect and keep his own. Nor are his followers unworthy of their chief; when he is slain, they fight on as before, undismayed, while the very soul of bravery speaks in Byrhtwold's noble words, "Courage should be the greater, the more our forces lessen."

Although the imperial power was inferior to the royal, from the feudal point of view, still the emperor held the power of the Roman name, a name which yet stood for the mightiest empire men had known, and for the language, law, and learning of the West; again, he held the power of the Christian name, and as "Protector of the Catholic Faith" could demand the service and homage of all Christian men. In this latter regard, however, he was the inferior of the pope, who was proved to be the strongest force in the Empire by the bitter strife of Hildebrand and Henry. How thoroughly the Empire was regarded as a sort of "church militant" is shown by the imperial title, which clearly marks the imperial office as that of a general of the faith, and by the fact that new peoples could only enter the Empire by acknowledging themselves the subjects of the church.[2] While the church claimed a peculiar right to the imperial service, still in the call to the crusades the popes claimed a right to the arms of all Christendom in defense of the Christian faith, a claim which was not denied though often neglected. In fact, the boundary of civilized Europe was one with the boundary of Christian Europe. Throughout Europe the church was still the

---

[1] Note the traces of Teutonic organization in this unit; the loyalty to a loved chief; the kinship bond; the duty of vengeance.

[2] Compare the case of Normans in France, who were, like the Hungarians, allowed to settle on condition of accepting Christianity. The weakness of civilized Europe is indicated by the fact that in both cases the invaders seize and hold most desirable territory.

prime civilizer; the monasteries were still the centres of learning and authorship; Gerbert gave an impulse to science and mechanical industry; the archbishops taught and advised the monarchs; as new peoples were assimilated, they were persuaded to the habits as well as the creed of Christianity; thus in Bulgaria we see the church opposing polygamy, superstition, and cruelty.

Although there is little that is striking in the intellectual life of this age, there is much that is significant, since tendencies then began which culminated only in the Renaissance; the Greek influence entered the West; the courts of England and France became intellectual centres; in England, France, and Spain national subjects or national languages appeared in literature, and Italy already began to gain artistic and scientific leadership. Europe, however, was still too harassed by invasion, too confused by feudalism, to permit of great results in scholarship or thought; her greatest names were still of warlike kings and chiefs, among whom the Normans appeared preeminent.

Attention should be called to the fact that the Moorish civilization, which culminated in this age, was developed along lines marked out from the first. The Arabs were the latest heirs of the wisdom of the East as modified by the Alexandrian influences; they were the mediæval authorities in astronomy, medicine, mathematics, and the Aristotelian philosophy; but their own authorities were confessedly Ptolemy, Galen, Hippocrates, Euclid, and Aristotle.

It is of the greatest interest to note how, in St. Mark's and the Ducal Palace all influences built themselves in marble; Greek and Oriental columns, Roman and Gothic arches, Oriental domes, Moorish ornament and color, all combined into a new beauty, neither Gothic, classic, nor Oriental, but Venetian, a beauty rich in detail and daring in cosmopolitan combination.

Suggestions for Essay and Examination Work. — The political power of a belief or myth, as illustrated by the "Holy Roman Empire." The "Marches" of the Empire. Of what use was the short-lived empire of Charlemagne? The influence of foreign invasion or attack upon internal unity, as illustrated in the English and German history of this age. How a baron spent the day, 900 A.D. Same of a serf; a bishop; a king. What were the elements of Otto's power? What progress has been made by the barbarians during this age? The losses of Constantinople. Alfred the Great and Charlemagne. The Norman war-chiefs. A group at Charlemagne's court. What characters of the period had lives that deserve the term "romantic"? Life in Normandy, 1000 A.D. The nobility of the age. Journal of Greek sent on an embassy to Bagdad. Gerbert in Spain.

B. STUDY ON CRUSADING PERIOD.

This study should be opened by a class conversation along the lines indicated by the questions on p. 318. The word "divisions," in the first of these questions, refers to the feudal divisions indicated on the map, and named in the key, in the upper left-hand corner; the most casual glance at them will show how feudalism had cut Western Europe into many petty little states, without specially natural boundaries; nor will the teacher, perhaps, find a more suitable time than this in which to call attention to the natural boundaries of the various European states, and to the fact that countries like England, Spain, Italy, and France, become more quickly consolidated and defined than countries like Germany, which has no well-defined natural barrier eastward, and so must depend the more on fortresses and arms.

If the teacher find himself behindhand with his work, but has been thorough with the preceding period, he may pass over this study very sketchily and hastily, since much of the work consists in the application to new circumstances of tendencies and organizations with which the student is already familiar. But enough attention must be given so that the relation of the crusades to the earlier and later mediæval period may not be missed. As the Persian wars were to Greece, and the Punic wars to Rome,

STUDY ON CRUSADING PERIOD. 95

so were the crusades to mediæval Europe, — an enlarging, enlivening movement, which brought young peoples into contact with ancient civilizations.

Throughout his study the student should be encouraged to summarize his own results as far as possible. But this sort of work is rather difficult, and, with most classes, the teacher will find it well to watch his opportunity to give practice on easily classified material, such as the crusades furnish. He may ask his pupils to tabulate their work on the crusades, under the following heads: COMPARISON OF ANTAGONISTS, CAUSES AND MOTIVES, LEADERS AND INSTIGATORS, ROUTES, LEADING EVENTS, RESULTS, USES AND EFFECTS. The results reached by the study on the whole period, however, will need a longer and more complex summary; the following may serve as a guide: —

CRUSADING PERIOD.

New Organizations and States formed.
    *a*Orders of knighthood.[1]
    Latin [2] kingdoms of East, —
        Jerusalem.
        Edessa.
    Latin [2] Empire of Constantinople.
    Lombard League (of Italian cities).[3]

Relative Conditions of Various European Powers.
    Papal and ecclesiastical power strengthening, seen in
        leadership and direction of crusades.[4]
            delegation of temporal power to ecclesiastics by crusaders.

---

[1] Those points marked "*a*" are expected to be obtained from the material, pp. 325–329.

[2] The use of this adjective "Latin" in connection with these new Eastern states is an incidental proof of the way in which the men of the West were still regarded as belonging to the *Latin* half of the Roman Empire.

[3] Notable as the first important example of these city-leagues, so influential in the later mediæval history of the Empire.

[4] This leadership gave the pope, for the time being, command of new material forces of men and money.

CRUSADING PERIOD. — *Continued.*
    "Concordat of Worms," and other papal victories in Germany.
    interference in temporal affairs, as in
        conquest of Ireland.
        quarrel of John of England with his barons.
    continued monopoly of art and literature.
  Imperial power weakening, seen in
    "Concordat of Worms."
    new and successful opposition of cities, —
        Italy.
        Germany.
    battle of Bouvines.
  Royal power strengthening in France,[1] through
    union of king and people against barons (note *Bouvines*).
    acquisition of new land by king.[2]
  Development of municipal power, seen in
    successful strife of cities with emperor.
    burgher victory of Bouvines.

Characteristics of Age.
  French leadership in crusades.[3]
  Uneasiness under papal and ecclesiastical rule, seen in
    strife of Guelph and Ghibelin.
    attempt of Arnold of Brescia.

---

[1] The royal power was also growing stronger in England, but not so evidently, since what had been gained against the pope and barons by preceding kings, was temporarily lost by John.

[2] Normandy would, in any case, have finally come to France, to which it naturally belonged, both by geographical position, and by unity of speech and general civilization.

[3] The French became the natural leaders of the crusades, because there was no serious disaffection in France against the pope, such as had been developed in Germany by the investiture quarrels; moreover, the French were the oldest and most securely Christianized people of the West, not even excepting Italy, since the Normans in the South, and the Lombards in the North, were later acquisitions to the faith than the warriors of Clovis. The fact of their predominance in the crusades finds an interesting confirmation in the Eastern use of the name "Frank" for all Europeans.

investiture quarrels in
> Germany.
> France.
> England.

heresies of Southern France, —
> Albigenses; Waldenses.

affair of Thomas Beket.

Gradual loss of crusading energy,
> seen in
>> indifferent or irrelevant results of later crusades.
>> greater inducements offered to later crusaders (see p. 332).
>> doubt felt at Antioch.
>
> caused by
>> ill success in East.
>> growing acquaintance with dangers and difficulties of undertaking.
>> loss of horror for the Infidel.

Constant contact of Greek, Oriental (*Moorish*), and Latin civilizations.

° Growth of intellectual energy,
> ° centering at
>> Paris (Abelard).
>> Cordova (Averroës).
>> Bologna.
>> monasteries.
>
> ° seen in
>> widening circle of intellectual interest, —
>>> theology.
>>> law.
>>> medicine.
>>> philosophy.
>>> history.
>>
>> growth of French as a literary language.

Tendencies of Crusading.

To weaken feudalism through
> unredeemed mortgages on feudal land,
> destruction of knights in crusades, ∴
> relative weakness of noble class in numbers, tending

CRUSADING PERIOD. — *Continued.*
> To strengthen
>> kings.
>> cities.
>> church (increasing its property by mortgaged or deeded lands of crusaders).
>
> To create new routes and demands for trade.
> To increase knowledge, —
>> geographical.
>> commercial and industrial.
>> historical.
>
> To introduce Oriental products and luxuries to the West.
> To increase respect for and value of industrial pursuits and artisan class.

If the teacher choose, he may add still another heading, EFFECTS OF CRUSADING; this, however, can only be filled out after the student has done the work on the later mediæval period. (See p. 111 of this manual.)

On comparing the West and the East at the opening of the crusades, it is easy to see that the West was comparatively still uncivilized; in the military art, the siege of Antioch had much to teach the crusaders, who were as yet unaccustomed to invest walled cities; in comparing the various captures of Jerusalem by Omar, by the first crusaders, and by Saladin, the Moslems are seen to be the more humane;[1] while the impressions of the astonished crusaders show how unaccustomed they were to the aspect of cultivated lands, and of cities strongly-built and adorned with the beauties of art.

From this astonishment the Venetians were exempt, accustomed as they were to trade eastward; to them, the crusades gave a chance for a great speculation, from which they gained

---

[1] Some excuse may be found for the crusaders in the general hostility of all Christians against the Jews, as being the people at whose hands Christ suffered death. It was evidently the belief of many of the first crusaders that it was a part of their duty to massacre these unfortunate people, wherever found.

not only new wealth and territory, but also a chance to plunder from Constantinople some of those "monuments" whose value they understood somewhat better than did their rude companions. It is significant of their long trading habits that they furnished neither men, money, nor ships, "for the love of God," without due recompense in pay or booty; and their bargain with the crusaders would show how considerable and wealthy a power Venice had already become, even if the rich beauty of St. Mark's and the Ducal Palace did not furnish material evidence of the fact.

The whole story of Thomas Beket, to its every detail, is very significant of the age; the main facts, given on p. 323, show at once the legal and political influence of churchmen, and the tendency of the age to revolt against this temporal power where it clashed with national government and unity; while in Beket's saintship and Henry's penance we see the still predominating hold of the spiritual power of Rome. But, strong as the church was growing, developing along the lines marked out by Gregory, it is significant that the revolts against her grew more frequent and daring, although, as yet, their most serious effort was to check her assertion of legal and political power. Intellectual revolt was still rare, and when it appeared, as in Southern France, was speedily suppressed in the interests of that unity of belief so essential to the papal power.

The appeals of Pope Urban, and still more the Papal Bull issued for the second crusade, are convincing proof that the crusading energy was due in part to other motives than those derived from desires to avenge the enslaved, persecuted, or murdered pilgrims, save Jerusalem from the infidel, and make of Palestine a Christian kingdom. That these motives were strong is seen in the enthusiasm with which Urban's appeal to them was met; but they were strengthened by the love of adventure, the passion of warfare, the hope of salvation, the desire for plunder, the charm of license, and in many cases, perhaps, by the power which was given to escape from the burdens of debt and the legal consequences of crime. On Saladin's side, also, the motives were undoubtedly mixed; but that they had a strong element of religious fervor, is clearly to be felt from Saladin's letter (p. 334).

The power of faith, even when it appears in the form of superstition, receives a striking illustration from the story of the "Sacred Lance," which, for the time being, served as well as if it had had genuine supernatural virtue, inasmuch as it gave absolute confidence, and all the strength which such a confidence inspires, to the weary and doubting crusaders.

The whole period is marked by no great distinguishing tendency or characteristic; it is a time of action in which old forms and ideas are tried, while new ones are suggested, — an age at once of culmination and of obscure, but originating change.

Suggestions for Essay and Examination Work. — The geographical advantages of England. The geographical disadvantages of Poland. Reflections of a Bulgarian upon the crusaders. Journal of a follower of Godfrey of Boulogne. The Christianity of Saladin. A French crusader's account of the taking of Antioch. Richard the Lion-heart, considered as an English king. When was the whole Roman Empire under "barbarian" rule? How would a crusader have justified the massacre of the Jews? What would be the natural relation of Moslems and Jews? What facts given in lists, pp. 325–329, prove this relation to have existed? Proofs that the civilization of the West was still *Roman*.

C. LATER MEDIÆVAL PERIOD, 1215-1492.

The following summary embodies the general results to be obtained from the studies on this period: —

LATER MEDIÆVAL PERIOD.

Organizations of Period.
    Feudal kingdoms growing into centralized national units by
        increase of royal power (consolidation and enlargement of royal domains).
        summoning to one place and for one purpose the assemblies of estates, —
            nobles.
            clergy.
            commons, —
                merchants (in England and on the continent).
                landed proprietors outside the noble class (in England).
        formation of national codes, —
            St. Lewis.
            Edward I.
            Alfonso of Castile.
        foreign wars: *ex.* Spanish wars with Moors, wars of English and French.
    The Empire[1] (Italy and Germany) greatly weakened and disintegrated by
        grants to nobles and clergy.
        strife of Guelph and Ghibelin.
        "great interregnum."
        loss of Poland.
        loss of Sicily.
        formation of Swiss league.
        formation of city leagues against nobles, —
            Hanse.
            Rhine.

---

[1] The imperial name at this time furnishes an excellent illustration of a "*dignity*," since it still held the respect of men by its antiquity, associations, and traditions, while all its real power was rapidly vanishing.

LATER MEDIÆVAL PERIOD. — *Continued.*
    wars and disturbances throughout Germany.
    wars and leagues of Italian cities.
The church, thoroughly centralized hierarchy, culminating in papal office, —
    powerful through
        unity, obtained by
            persecution of heresy (Inquisition).
            censorship of literature.
            independence of secular courts and imperial election.[1]
        wealth (note cathedrals).
        command of military orders.
        command of learning.
        judicial power.
        presence in assemblies of estates (political power).
        privilege and rank (the untaxed *second estate*).
        electoral nature of papacy.[2]
    threatened by
        "Schism of the West."
        growing tendency to heresy.
        growing dissatisfaction, most pronounced in Germany and England, with ecclesiastical government, doctrine, and morality, seen in
            attitude of kings.
            German electors.
            popular literature.
            Lollard and Hussite movement.
            heresies.
The guilds, democratic, local, co-operative societies of the third estate (merchants and artisans), —
    formed for
        mutual protection and aid.
        advancement of trade, ∴
    favorable to
        morality, peace, public health and cleanliness, high standard of workmanship, and

---

[1] Since the papal election was transferred to the College of Cardinals.
[2] The papal office was thus freed from the chances of birth and the family quarrels to which an ordinary monarchy is subject.

opposed to
- monopolies.
- inequality of advantage or opportunity.

united by bonds of
- mutual interest.
- kinship (often).[1]

The towns, democratic,[2] local governments,
- power based on *wealth*.
- bonds of union,
  - common local interests.
  - common residence.
- opposed to
  - irregular, arbitrary, and outside interference in local affairs.
- favoring
  - local independence.
  - trade.

Orders of knighthood.
- Their duties, —
  - to defend the church ⎫
  - to defend the king ⎬ military.
  - to defend the weak and defenceless ⎭
  - to hold to the Christian faith ⎫
  - to be loyal to their king ⎪ spiritual
  - to do justice ⎬ and
  - to be honorable, courteous, brave, ⎪ social.
  - humble, truthful, persevering ⎭

Characteristics of Period Special to England.

Prosperity of farming gentry (stock-farmers, raising sheep), seen in
- presence in third estate.
- tax on wool.

Successful establishment of constitution (compare with result of constitutional struggle in France), embodied in

---

[1] The guild privileges were freely open to the sons and daughters of guildsmen; the trades thus became largely hereditary.

[2] *Within the body of citizens,* democracy was the ruling principle; but this body could not be said to include men of what has been called the fourth estate.

Later Mediæval Period. — *Continued.*
  Great Charter, demanding [1]
    "No taxation without representation."
    jury trial (judgment by peers).
    "Habeas corpus" (no delay in justice).

Characteristics Special to France.
  Strife of king and towns and nobles, ending in
    victory of king over nobles, and accompanied by
      steady enlargement of royal domain.[2]
    substitution of king's law for
      trial by battle and arbitrary judgments.
  Close relations with papacy, seen in
    papal offer of Sicily to Anjou.
    removal of papal seat to Avignon.

Characteristics Special to Spain.
  Superior strength of royalty (large domain).

Characteristics General through Western Europe.
  Growing prosperity of middle trading-classes, seen in
    formation and powers of third estate,
    formation and powers of guilds,
    buildings and defenses of towns;
    political and military power of towns, evinced in
      Flemish and Parisian revolts.
      wars of Italian towns.
      formation of powerful leagues.
    taxes imposed on third estate (wool-tax in England).
    growing prominence of manufacturing industries.
  Growth of nationalities, displaying itself in differentiation of
    language, history,[3] intellectual interest, and in codification of national law.

---

[1] These demands indicate the directions in which Englishmen had felt oppression.

[2] This enlargement, of course, under the "Old Régime," meant the enlargement of the king's resources. Here we see the special reason why the desire for territorial possession should be the moving cause of the long wars of the French and English kings.

[3] It will be noted that, from the time of the crusades on, the history of Europe cannot be treated in the *mass*, since each country begins its own proper development.

Strife of the nearly balanced powers of towns, kings, nobles,
   popes, resulting in
      multiplicity of defenses,[1] —
         castles.
         town walls.
      victories of towns and princes in
         Germany and Italy.
      royal victory in France.
      general instability and insecurity.
Growth of popular [2] liberty (as a purpose or a fact),
   seen in
         growth of electoral principle in
            towns.
            guilds.
            College of Cardinals.
            electors of Empire.
         attempts at political independence or liberty, —
            Cola di Rienzi.
            Marcel.
            demands of estates
               in England, France, and Spain.
         increase of local freedom (towns).
         participation of all classes in literary and artistic
            movements.
   favored by
         needs of kings for money from the third estate.
         growing intelligence of people.
Social uneasiness and agitation among those of the lowest class
   (fourth estate).
      seen in
         Jacquerie.
         Wat Tyler's revolt.
         Hussite War.

---

[1] Compare with the standing armies of the nearly balanced powers of Europe to-day.

[2] It must, however, be remembered that the word "popular" does not apply to men below the station of the third estate.

LATER MEDIÆVAL PERIOD. — *Continued.*
    Intellectual and artistic activity among all classes.[1]
        seen in
            literature $\begin{cases} \text{poetry} \\ \text{history} \\ \text{travels} \end{cases}$, Italy and England leading.
            theology and philosophy, France leading.
            science, Italy leading, —
                confused.
                undifferentiated.
                aiming at
                    prolonging life and renewing youth.
                    changing other metals to gold.
                    foretelling the future.
                laying foundations for
                    chemistry $\Big\}$ (alchemy).
                    mineralogy
                    astronomy (astrology).
            painting and sculpture (led by Italy and Germany), —
                original[2] in subject (Biblical).
            architecture (led by France and Germany), —
                original
                    in structure (pointed arch, *Gothic*).
                    in decoration (stained glass).
                influenced by
                    Greek, Roman, and Moorish forms.
            learning (universities), Italy and France leading.
            heresies.
            inventions.
        patronized by
            church,
            princes, and
            wealthy merchants.

---

[1] Here, as in political life, "all classes" refers to the three estates, the lowest class not yet appearing as an intellectual or social element in the state.

[2] Following out the lines indicated by the early church.

influenced by
- Moors, in science, philosophy, and art.
- Greeks, in science, philosophy, and art.
- Romans, in law and literature.

rendered influential and general by
- printing and engraving.
- comforts and contrivances for giving men leisure, comfort, and quiet.

characterized by
- European interchange of thought and knowledge.
- versatility and variety.

Organization, — of tendencies, occupations, classes; of
- chivalry in knighthood.
- faith in new monastic orders.
- learning in universities.
- trades in guilds.
- classes and occupations in estates, —
  - nobles.
  - clergy.
  - third estate.

Centralization, — of feudalism in kings, of the church in papacy, of third estate in town organizations.

Growth of new ideals, —
- the knight.
- the "Doctor."
- the wealthy merchant.
- the author and artist.

It should be thoroughly understood that the assemblies of estates were quite different from our modern legislative bodies. The interests they represented were those of classes, not of the whole people; they were called together at the will of the monarch, and primarily in his interest, either because he wished their advice, their moral support, or their money. Naturally, then, they were composed of the rich, influential, and intelligent classes, and included the third estate, not as a matter of justice, but because this estate contained the wealthy merchants, and could bring to the royal service a heavy purse. Originating thus in the needs of the monarchs, the estates, especially the commons, found a means of enforcing attention to their claims, and of winning new privilege and political importance. In other words, the king often found himself obliged to buy their aid; thus, in England, he paid for it by charters, favors, and promises, tending to give wider liberties and juster government; in France, the history was the same, but there the king's strength finally proved superior to that of the estates; and thus, while in England, Magna Charta laid the foundation of constitutional government, in France the equally wise demands of Marcel and the Parisians ended in the triumph of royalty.

To the modern student, the subject of guilds is of especial interest, since it was the mediæval solution of the "labor problem," and a solution not merely successful, but brilliant. Their study is at once so easy and so suggestive, that the teacher will find in it an admirable place for much conversational work, such as would grow out of the question as to the value to the guildsmen of morality, peace, public health, and cleanliness. In talking this over, the teacher should be careful to keep in mind the *tradesman's* point of view; for each of these conditions had its own special value to the trader and artisan, as ensuring him quiet and favorable conditions for work, while at the same time they rendered his place of labor or residence secure and attractive to the buyer. For the same reasons we find that, in the assemblies of estates, the third estate always inclined to vote for peace rather than war.

The most vital point of the guild organizations was this: *they were built upon the principle of co-operative instead of upon that of competitive industry.* All the men of the same calling within the same town-walls, worked together for a common good, inspired by common interests, and by a common pride in the honor and excellence of the guild. Thus, in their relation to the outer world, they may be described as monopolists of labor, since no man could successfully follow any business outside the ranks of a guild; within those ranks, however, monopoly, and even a disproportionate command of men and other means of labor, were strictly prevented.

The power of the guilds evidently underlay that of the towns, those great mediæval fortresses of labor, whose increasing resources caused the comparative decline of the noble class, and acted as a check on needy kings, who were glad to buy the right of taxation with charters of liberty. These charters plainly show that the towns had suffered much from the arbitrary judgments and irregular interference of kings and nobles, and that liberty meant to them the power to judge and manage in regard to their own local affairs. Hence we see why the towns always favored the power of kings rather than that of nobles, since the former at least represented a central, standard authority.

The success of the trading-class, and the quickening of popular thought, could hardly fail to rouse the consciousness of the great "fourth estate," composed of untrained laborers. This class, both in England and in France, now first urged its way into notice by bloody, unintelligent, and ineffective revolt. There is an indication that this class was more intelligent in England than in France, in the fact that Wat Tyler and his followers appealed to the king as the fountain of justice, while the "Jacquerie" was a blind protest made in fire and murder; this, of course, is but conjecture, and I have called attention to the point chiefly for the sake of making the student realize the difference between an indication and a proof. But while revolt accomplished nothing for the poorest class of all, the "Black Death" did much to free man from the soil, and change the serf into a wage laborer.[1] At a moderate calculation, a third of the people perished by this plague; in consequence, labor was so scarce, that the surviving laborers were able to enforce their demands for money payments, or for higher wages. This movement is, however, important to

---

[1] The slave could be bought and sold at the will of his masters; the serf could only be bought or sold with the land which he cultivated, and the home where he lived; the wage laborer is bound neither to a man nor a field, but sells his labor as freely as the circumstances of the market permit.

notice, as a beginning of the long agitations of the laboring classes, rather than as a strong mark of this period.

Woven throughout the texture of European society, the ecclesiastical power saw itself threatened with dismemberment, as distinct nationalities began to gather about new centres, and Rome began to be forgotten as the common mother. The unity of the church, and its traditional relations to the temporal powers, was diametrically opposed to the formation of independent kingdoms within the body of Christendom; this, as well as the legal power of the church, and the ecclesiastical control of large amounts of land, threatened the peace and unity of states. Thus the inevitable conflict of the temporal with the spiritual power approached, and most rapidly in Germany, where the conflicting claims of pope and emperor had already caused centuries of conflict and confusion.

The whole period is marked by the strife of nearly balanced powers; but classes, rather than nations, were the opposing forces; the noble checked the king, and the town checked both, while obscure but significant movements were felt in still lower strata.

If "number is quality," then these centuries should rank high in human history for their great number of famous men. Not only is the list a long, but a varied one, and in this regard it contrasts curiously with the lists of the Christian Empire and the early mediæval period, which belong to a one-sided development correspondingly intense. Men were now trained for achievement not only in the cloister, but in the camp, the court, the workshop, and the studio; and it is interesting to note that, perhaps without exception, the training had a direct relation to the man's life-work.

Even before the invention of printing, the increasing wealth and culture of laymen is evidenced by the production of a great secular literature in the various national tongues of Europe; the subjects of this literature reflect the learning, the thought, the feeling of the age; and such a list as that of Caxton's first editions is an admirable index to the intellectual life of the time, since it gives a practical gauge of literary popularity.

This period is so alive and complete, so full of old powers waning and new ones waxing, that it is perhaps impossible to say, with any certainty, just what part of its new life Europe owed to the crusades; it is easy to reason out relations between these movements and the new impulses in science, art, and trade; but such reasoning must always be tempered by the memory of the Moors in Spain, and of the close relations of the East with Venice and the other great Italian marts.

In the study on p. 378, I have tried to show in some detail how pictures may be used in the study of history.

In *a*, *b*, *c*, *d*, we see an architecture quite different from that of Greece, or Rome, or the East; the spire, the pointed arch, the tower, have succeeded the pillar, the rounded arch, and the dome; the basis of decoration is found in the openings of the walls, in the windows and doors; stained glass has become an important material in decorative art, while its subjects are drawn from Christian scripture and tradition; in the portal (*c*) the forms employed are again the forms of human beings, as in the Greek temple, but the forms are now of saints, and not of athletes. And yet throughout we see the influence of the earlier civilizations; the Greek pillar, the Roman arch, the Moorish ornament, are all present, but modified and subordinated by a new spirit, expressing itself in an architecture essentially new. The most Gothic of these four pictures, the most purely original to this period, is, perhaps, *c*; and yet even there the presence of some little Greek pillars, used as part of the decoration, betrays the ineffaceable influence. As for the beauties of *a*, *b*, *c*, and *d*, every one must judge for himself; such structures at least proclaim the wealth of the church, and its close relation with and command over the artistic resource of the age.

The castles, as well as the cathedrals, bear their witness. Comparing *e* and *f* with Fountains Hall, p. 413, we realize at once that the world had suffered change between the days when a noble built his castle on a forbidding height, surrounded it by inhospitable moats, challenged all comers before giving them the narrow passage of the drawbridge, shut himself within thick walls, peeped suspiciously at the outside world through high and narrow slits, kept guard and watch on his castle towers,— and the days when this same knight made himself a pleasant house in the open country, with generous doors and windows, and surrounded it with the attractions of wood and field and garden; the castle was the necessary product of an age when each man stood on his own defence, while Fountains Hall was built in an age of kings, when the feudal quarrels had been suppressed, and the military resources of the country were massed in a single hand, thus rendered strong enough to keep the peace, and enable men to live more freely and carelessly than before.

The third estate, meanwhile, is represented by such noble guild-halls as that of Ypres, p. 377, which, were it our only evidence, would tell us of the wealth, importance, and taste of the merchant class, besides giving us a very good list of the industries of the age.

The study of laws often tells us quite as much of injustice as of justice: that is, a law generally tells us of some unjust or unfortunate state of affairs which it was intended to obviate. Thus, Magna Charta clearly indicates that the English king had made excessive and arbitrary demands for money, had seized men's property for his own use, had over-ridden the ancient liberties of the towns, had sold and delayed justice; that the nobles had unreasonably oppressed their retainers for more than the customary feudal dues; that no man was safe from arbitrary arrest and imprisonment, and that men were often condemned without a fair hearing. Magna Charta is sometimes represented as the work of the great nobles, but that it equally represented the third estate of free, untitled men, is proved by articles 20, 46, 48, p. 379. In the parallel French demands (p. 381) we see also the union of the nobles and commons against the arbitrary power of the king.

In extracts *b* and *d*, pp. 380, 381, we see the royal power evidently directed to quell the power and violence of the nobles, and for this purpose allying itself with the commons of the realm; while *e*, p. 382, shows the result of this struggle in establishing a monarchy possessing unchecked control over the composition of the army and the raising of the taxes, and thus enabled to become a genuine absolutism. Thus, while England advances in political civilization, and finds herself possessed of advanced constitutional principles, tending to work themselves out in practical forms, France finds herself retrograding toward the simpler form of absolute monarchy.

The laws on p. 383 are rather indicative of social than political conditions; we see a state dependent for defense on the arms of its free citizens, acting as volunteers; a country still insecure, uncleared, and full of disorder; a city where all political power is in the hands of traders, while two of these ordinances throw a curious light on the sincere interest and belief of the age in the experiments of alchemy.

The literature of this period indicates clearly enough that its wrongs and abuses sprang chiefly from two classes, the aristocratic and the clerical; the nobles were the oppressors, — the monks, the scandals of the age; the arbitrary, petty wars, the confused and unequal laws, which had their origin among the former, the extravagance, luxury, and immorality of the latter, called forth much complaint and invective, humorously voiced by Chaucer, but sternly by Dante, whose feeling was intensified by his identification with the Ghibelins[1] in the long mediæval strife of papal and imperial powers.

Chaucer gives us the picture and the temper of the later mediæval period, while Dante gives us its serious feeling and thought. In the extracts, pp. 386–388, the condition of the Holy Roman Empire is vividly set forth. We see at once that, in Dante's mind, the ancient union still existed; but that its ruinous condition was attributed to the imperial neglect of Italy and the seizure of the temporal power by Rome.

---

[1] In his youth Dante had been a Guelph.

In the extracts from Chaucer we see how thoroughly the early mediæval saint ideal of the church had given way to desires for politeness, culture, pleasure, and luxury; while the warrior ideal of the Teuton has softened to the "very perfect, gentle knight," in fact, to the ideal "*gentleman*" and the gay young squire, thoroughly trained for the graceful accomplishments of the court, as well as the strenuous duties of the field.[1]

If the teacher himself regard this age a "dark" one, he may find means of impressing this opinion on the minds of his pupils; to my own view, it appears as one of the most rapidly-moving and important of historical epochs. While England led in politics, Italy in art, and France in courtesy and material elegance, still the whole of Europe "marched," its various states essentially abreast.

Suggestions for Examination and Essay Work. — The guild and the trades-union; their resemblances and differences. The assemblies of estates and modern representative chambers. Review the development of papacy. The town aristocrats. Why should the trading classes desire the suppression of the nobility? What were the great historic sources of the civilization of this period. Why should the houses in European towns, dating back to the fourteenth and fifteenth centuries, be so built that the people must live in the second and third stories; and why should the streets of those same towns be so narrow? What reasons would a man living in the fifteenth century have for thinking the ruin of Europe near? What reasonable grounds might he see for improvement? Journal of a Parisian merchant living in the first half of the fifteenth century. Same of a French noble. Same of an English wool-grower for latter half of the same century. The advantages of kings to trade. Wiclif and St. Francis of Assisi compared as reformers. The debt of the later mediæval period to Rome. To Greece and the Orient. The secularization of the church. A day in the castle of Pierrefond. "Piper's day" at castle St. Ulric. The mediæval *versus* the Greek beauty.

---

[1] Compare the list of the squire's accomplishments with the list now required for an "accomplished" young lady. In both cases the education is a social one.

D. REFORMATION AND RENAISSANCE ERA.

The general results of the studies in this period may be thus summarized: —

REFORMATION AND RENAISSANCE, 1492-1648.

Great Movements and Achievements of the Time.
    Geographical discovery, —
        eastward, led by Portugal.
        westward, led by Spain.
    caused by
        desire to discover routes to India.
        desire to gain new landed possessions.
    resulting in
        circumnavigation of Africa.
        foundation of European colonies in India.
        discovery and settlement of America.
        development of maritime powers, —[1]
            Holland.
            Spain.
            Portugal.
            England.
            France.
        great increase of commercial activity.
        change of commercial centre from Mediterranean to Atlantic,[2] ∴.
        decay of Italian commerce.

---

[1] Note that Spain held as strong a command over all the westward commerce of the Mediterranean as Constantinople over that of the Black Sea; this, combined with her own free access to transatlantic shores, made her one of the leaders of the new commerce. Without this command, France, Portugal, England, and Holland had the freedom of access; and in the case of Holland, her connection with Spain during the period of discovery very probably gave her her first commercial experience and impulse, strengthened by her own half-maritime life and the poverty of her internal resources.

[2] The opening of the Suez Canal in our own time may tend to restore the commercial activity of the Mediterranean lands.

REFORMATION AND RENAISSANCE. — *Continued.*

Revolt against the church,
  caused or favored by
    intellectual dissent from her doctrines
      (England and Europe in general).
    desire of monarchs for entire independence
      (England).
    disapproval of her methods and morals
      (Germany and Europe in general).
    internal corruption, —
      avarice.
      luxury.
      immorality.
      ignorance.
    mediæval quarrels of church and state ⎱ Germany.
    independence of Teutonic character ⎰
  resulting in
    formation of national churches.
    formation of various Protestant sects.
    internal reform (the Jesuit movement).

Production of masterpieces, —
  in painting, Italy, Germany.
  in dramatic literature, England.

Overthrow of the feudal monarchy in England,
  caused by
    taxation without representation.[1]
    intolerance toward dissenting sects.[1]
  For results, see next period (note colonizations).

Facts of Organization.

Formation of the strong centralized feudal monarchies of the "Old Régime"
  in France.
  in England.
  in Spain.

---

[1] The first of these grievances evidently antedated Magna Charta; while the second began to be oppressive under Elizabeth; constitutional measures on the part of the king, and tolerance on the part of the people, might have averted the Civil Wars.

brought about by
- consolidation of lands in royal hands, through
  - inheritance.
  - conquest.
  - marriage.
- formation of standing armies.
- common interests of king and people in
  - religion.
  - commerce.

Formation of independent national churches in
- England.
- Scotland.
- Switzerland.
- various German states.

Formation of national units (France, England, Spain),
- bound togther by
  - language.
  - faith.
  - loyalty to a single king.
  - common interests of natural geographical units.
- represented by national, hereditary monarchs.

Foundation of extra-European, Christian colonies
- in Asia.
- in America.

Weakness and disintegration of the Empire,[1]
- seen in
  - difficulty in quelling peasants' war.
  - territorial gains of France and Spain, at the expense of the Empire,
    - along the Rhine.
    - in Italy.
  - sovereign political power held by *princes*.
  - peace of Westphalia.
- caused by
  - inherent weakness of imperial office.
  - dissensions of Catholics and Protestants.

---

[1] Under Charles the Fifth, who was such an extensive land-owner by his ancestral heritages, the Empire temporarily revived.

Reformation and Renaissance. — *Continued.*

    culminating in
      Thirty Years' War.
      imperial loss of
        Switzerland.
        Holland.[1]
      loose confederation of sovereign states, nominally under the emperor.

Characteristics of the Age.

  Leading interests, religion, and trade, seen in

    causes of war } ; see { civil wars of France, Germany, England. "Great Armada." Thirty Years' War. } treaties of peace

    objects of Columbus and other explorers.
    missionary enterprise.
    religious intolerance.
    literary productions, —
      translations of Bible.
      popular satires.
    artistic subjects.
  Change of the noble from a military to a courtly and cultured class, caused by
      massing of political and military power in royal hands.
      employment of gunpowder and standing armies.
    resulting in
      their appearance in
        literature.
        art.
        adventure.[2]
      use of feudal wealth in art and display.
  Dissatisfaction of the fourth estate, seen in
    German peasant wars.
    outcry against enclosures in England.

---

[1] Italy went piecemeal, being common booty for France, Spain, and Austria, from the opening of the sixteenth century till the days of Victor Emmanuel.

[2] Note the early leaders of discovery.

Intense and varied intellectual activity, seen in
> Reformation movement.
> revival of learning, —
>> Latin language and literature.
>> Greek language and literature.
>>> favored by Reformation.[1]
> new forms of literature, —
>> drama.
>> essay.
>> romance.
> revolt against, Aristotle[2] in
>> Platonic movement.
>> inductive philosophy of Bacon.
> study of natural science.[2]
> appeal to reason and observation as bases of truth.[2]

Increase of domestic comfort and safety.
Strong influence of classic antiquity, seen in
> art.
> education.
> literature (translations, imitations, themes).

International action and reaction, seen in
> international wars.
> importation or travel of artists from country to country.
> translations.[8]
> Italian influence
>> in English literature.[8]
>> on French manufacture.

---

[1] The same intellectual impulse which urged men to the study of nature in science, urged them to the study of the Greek and Hebrew originals in theology. (See Luther's letter, p. 424.)

[2] The first two statements are in reality but particulars under the third, which marks the age in religion, art, and thought. The *original source*, be it the revealed truth, the natural form, or the untranslated classic, is the object of desire. In this desire, Italy herself led, though it was beyond her power to achieve.

[8] The translations of the great works of antiquity and of the Middle Age undoubtedly had their influence in unifying Europe, since they gave her a common body of literary material from which to start, — an influence greatly facilitated by the new invention of printing, which likewise quickened the influence of one country on another, as of Italy on England,

It has been the custom, in many of our text-books, to date the beginning of modern history at 1453, or at 1492; but although new elements then appear, still the great events, the characteristic forms of the Renaissance, seem to be the culmination of the whole feudal, mediæval period. From the long struggles of king and baron, strong-handed monarchies emerged; from the long quarrels of temporal and spiritual powers within the Empire, and the long-felt intellectual revolt against an ancient, detailed creed, the Reformation sprang; Columbus was the greatest of a line of daring Italian travellers and navigators who prepared his way; in Raphael and Michael Angelo, bloomed the Christian art which Italy had never failed to cherish through all her mediæval confusion.[1]

Meanwhile, the absolutely new, the modern impulses that began in these centuries did not characterize them, but awaited their development in a later era. For these reasons, then, it has seemed best not to use the word "modern" until 1648 be passed, and to treat this period as the climax of that Catholic and feudal civilization which had slowly formed the states of Europe during the mediæval age; the more so since such a view gives significance and meaning to all the struggles, imperfections, and confusions necessary to develop the strong, clear forms of the sixteenth century.

In comparing the map on p. 397 with that on pp. 316, 317, the most striking changes noted are the respective enlargement of the French and Spanish territories, and the obliteration of their feudal divisions; this at once tells the story of the royal strength within their boundaries, and their appearance as fully formed *national country-states*, as opposed to the *tribal city-states* of antiquity. Here, again, the teacher should enforce the point, that landed possession lay at the foundation of all political and military power under the feudal system. Thus Charles the Fifth became the strongest monarch of his age,

---

[1] It must not be forgotten that Italy was, par excellence, the land of the church and the popes.

through his inheritance of family titles to European lands; although America was also included in his empire, still its unmanageable distance, and the fact that it was neither cultivated nor settled, and so unable to yield either taxes or troops, made it of little value as a basis of political power, although from the first it was a rich source of the raw materials of commerce.¹ From this desire for land, Italy was the greatest sufferer; divided among many petty powers, incapable of union, and yet too strong to be subdued, under the nominal rule of an emperor who had more than he could rightly manage on the northern side of the Alps, — Italy was, as Dante named her, an "inn of grief"; indeed, the events of the sixteenth century (c) show that her possession was one of the great ambitions common to the European powers or, to speak more justly, to the European monarchs, for within this age, the monarchs were indeed the powers of Europe, with their standing armies and consolidated territories. Proof of this is seen in the arbitrary rule of Philip the Second of Spain, of Francis the First in France, of Henry the Eighth of England. Nothing more thoroughly displayed their strength than their ability to deal absolutely with the strongest interest of the age, religious faith, and to impose at will the Catholic or Protestant creed upon their subjects;² the same fact shows how thoroughly the monarchies embodied the spirit of centralization, of national unity, and it may perhaps be argued that the high-handed intolerance with which Jews and Moors were driven from Spain, Huguenots massacred in France, Dissenters suppressed in England, was a historic necessity in the formation of self-sustaining national units.³ considering how

---

¹ To France and England, America soon added to this advantage that of serving as an asylum for religious refugees.

² In France, their difficulty was enhanced by the fact that the religious parties revived the historic antagonism of king and noble.

³ One must not say too much, however, on this point, unless he wishes logically to find himself on the side of Bismarck, in his attempt to drive the Poles from Prussian Poland. In illustration, however, of the royal side of the question, see Queen Elizabeth's letter, p. 432.

high the feeling ran between men of opposing creeds. Thus the censorship of the press was felt almost from the beginning to be a necessity both by the pope, and by the various absolute monarchs, since their centralized powers depended too thoroughly on men's universal approval to render wide-spread intellectual dissent and free discussion safe. To the centralization of wealth and power in the hands of their kings, the countries of Western Europe owed, however, much of their material and commercial progress. In England, France, and Spain, the court was the centre of impulse for discovery, colonization, art, and literature. If the teacher have the time, he will find that a very valuable sub-study may be made in this connection of Queen Elizabeth, whose reign displayed absolutism, perhaps, at its best, although its more objectionable features were not so much absent as overshadowed.[1] In the reign of James the First, on the contrary, these were the more decided features; the expenses of the court devoured the earnings of the land which in justice should have been spent for the good of its people (see member for Oxford's speech, p. 433); taxes had been imposed without consent of Parliament; worst of all, the king attempted to suppress the free speech of its members. It was the old feudal contest with the old feudal weapons all over again; the king was poor, and must have money from his estates, who, on their part, would grant nothing without concessions of justice from the king. In the debate accompanying the Petition of Right, pp. 433, 434, it is plainly evident that men's minds yet clung to the feudal theory of a king's support, and felt that he should meet his own expenses from his own domain, the modern system of paying him a regular annual sum from a civil service list, whose charges are met by popular taxes, not yet having been invented.

---

[1] At least he should stop to note, that as a strong and noble nationality calls forth the ardent patriotism of its citizens, so a strong, wise, truly "paternal" monarch calls forth the warm loyalty of his subjects (see *i* and *j*, p. 430).

These causes of the English civil wars, however, would seem to have been subordinate to those arising from religious dissent; judging from Hobbes' "Leviathan," and the "Solemn League," this was the cause which drove men on to war.

The Scots' "Solemn League and Covenant" is one of the most significant documents of the age; it breathes a solemn biblical intensity of faith; it holds by an absolute union of church and state, in which the state shall be composed of the church, with the king for its executive servant;[1] it is of necessity intolerant of Catholics and members of the established church. In all these ways it reflects the spirit and thought of the time, from the Puritan point of view, as Hobbes' "Leviathan" reflects it from the Royalist standpoint.

It is generally felt that the Reformation is a rather delicate subject to deal with, so closely does it touch our own living interests. It is true that the movement is too often solely regarded from the Protestant standpoint, and explained exclusively as a great theological revolution. But a comparison of the decrees of the Council of Trent and of the Augsburg Confession will show that the theological differences were minor, while the practical questions of the marriage of priests and the relation of church and state were revolutionary; the Protestant position of a "free church in a free state" was indeed so opposed to the whole European system from the earliest times, that not even the Protestants themselves knew how in that age to achieve it. Moreover, a due remembrance of the tendencies and facts of later mediæval history will show that the Reformation was the inevitable culmination of the secularization of the church, of national revolt against centralization, of intellectual revolt against authority. Luther came in the "fulness of time," the successor of Wiclif and Huss, and with a body of long-gathering popular favor to sustain him. The facts that

---

[1] Compare Cowell's "Interpreter," where the king is regarded as the source of law and above the law; in the Puritan and Scotch view, the king is but the executive of fixed law.

the strongest spirits of the age were his upholders or forerunners, that half the people of Europe were his admirers or followers, and that for more than a century the questions voiced so boldly by Luther shook Europe with war, prove clearly that he was a representative man, a man who spoke for half the world, a necessary man, demanded by the stress of contemporary thought and feeling. If time and circumstance favor, the teacher can make a most admirable character study on Luther, whose power largely consisted in his honesty, directness, independence, and passionate love of truth. Even in the extracts given, pp. 423, 424, it is plainly to be seen that he was eminently a conservative, and that his respect for the authority of the church was only exceeded by loyalty to the best truth he could discern.

That the church was in need of reformation was clearly proved by the calling of the Council of Trent, and the earnest, wide-spread Jesuit movement; within her precincts occurred a true reform, whose effects have lasted to the present time; while the so-called Reformation was more of the nature of a revolt, ending in the secession of the Teutonic races from that Latin church which had claimed to be the head and heart of Christendom. So thoroughly, however, had the church made itself one with all the secular interests of Europe, that this secession could only be accomplished either through great political disturbance, or by an appeal to arms; and even then, as seen in the peace of Augsburg, it was still thought necessary for each prince to settle the religion of his own subjects; unjust as this seems to modern ideas, we must always remember that differences in religion then meant civil war. In fact, of the two leading interests of the age, religion and trade, religion was the stronger, as proved by the facts, that, in opposition to all commercial considerations, such useful industrial populations as the Huguenots in France, or the Moors in Spain, were expelled or massacred; while the ruling motive of the most important wars was decidedly religious difference. That this motive affected peoples as thoroughly as kings is proved by the fact that it was the motive of popular revolt and civil war as well as of international contest.[1] One of the most interesting and picturesque illustrations of this prevailing spirit of the age is to be seen in all the events connected with the Great Armada. Its first object purported to be the recovery of England from heresy; its second, to cripple forever a foe already felt to be dangerous to Spanish commerce and colonization. On the side of the English and Dutch, meanwhile, the strongest defence against this mighty fleet was believed to be national prayer, and its misfortune and defeat were felt to be surely due to divine interposition.

These wars of the Reformation essentially ended with the Thirty Years' War, one of the most important conflicts of modern times, not only on account of its magnitude and length, but because it made important changes on the European map; while, during its progress, religious differences wearied themselves out, or were settled with sufficient tolerance to render Europe quiet. It is significant to note in this connection, that France under the lead of Cardinal Richelieu already subordinated religious to political interests, since she entered the war on the side of the Protestants, in order still further to weaken her neighbor, the emperor, and disunite the Empire.

At the opening of the sixteenth century the kings of the West had pretty well escaped from the tyranny of the feudal nobles; not so the peasants. Their complaints in Alsace-Lorraine, and the account of their state given in More's Utopia, show that they had been deprived of their ancient use of the land, and of their old common rights to forest and waste, which they had inherited from their Teutonic ancestors. In England, the practice of the landlords of turning their lands into sheep-farms greatly injured the poorer agricultural class,

---

[1] In the Peasants' War, the program of the peasants clearly shows how thoroughly social and political change seemed to them the natural accompaniment of religious reform, since, in all their experience, these elements were inextricably involved in the consolidated structure under which they had always lived.

"for," as More says, "one shepherd . . . is enough to eat up that ground with cattle, to the occupying whereof about husbandry many hands were requisite." These "hands" being driven from their accustomed labor, unconsciously revenged themselves upon the state by becoming paupers, vagabonds, and thieves, thus changing from a valuable to a mischievous population; nor did the sheep-pastures help to ameliorate this state of things by cheapening any necessity of life, since the landlords were so wealthy and few that they easily monopolized the trade in wool, holding the prices where they would.

The discoveries of the period were as purely commercial in their character as any of its undertakings. Yet the letter of Columbus[1] (p. 421) shows how thoroughly zeal for the spread of the Catholic faith was mingled with the more secular objects of conquest and trade. From the very first, moreover, as is seen from the letter of Raleigh, national jealousies began to arise over these new-world possessions, England fearing lest Spain should become "unresistible" through these wealthy lands.

The special original art of the Renaissance was painting, an art which reflected the three strong intellectual tendencies of the age. It borrowed its subjects from religion; it sought its principles from Greek antiquity; it drew its immediate inspiration from the direct study of nature; these facts are illustrated by nearly every work of Raphael and Michael Angelo. In architecture, also, the antique forms appeared in the new combinations. In the court of the Borghese palace are mingled the Roman arch, the Greek pillar, and the mediæval statue, while in St. Peter's, a similar combination is overtopped by the Oriental dome. While it is to be noted in this connection, that

---

[1] If the teacher have the time and material at hand, he can make a most interesting study of Columbus, whose life and character embodied much of the circumstances and spirit of the age. Even in the extract given, we see the loyalty, zeal, and modesty of this wonderful man, who has become too much of a name "to conjure by," instead of being present to our minds as a genuine and noble reality.

the fine arts of the Renaissance owed their development to the patronage of courts and wealthy Italian merchants, still it must be remembered that opportunity and not inspiration was thus supplied.

Suggestions for Essay and Examination Work.—The map of Europe, the political picture of the age. General view of the unity of the church from 325 to 1648. The political view of the Reformation. The three emperors, Augustus, Charlemagne, and Charles the Fifth. Famous monks. Why did not Italy and Germany become feudal monarchies like France and Spain? "The ships of Tarshish." Was religious toleration, as we understand it, possible in the Reformation? (Debate.) In what ways was the Renaissance the culmination of mediæval civilization? The crimes of the sixteenth century. Extracts from the diary of a Protestant Dutchman, who emigrated to Manhattan Island. Same of an English Catholic emigrating to Maryland. The history embodied in the Escorial. Was patronage necessary to the development of the Renaissance art? How could literature become somewhat free from patronage in this age? How did the discovery of America affect religious energy. Bacon v. Aristotle. Effect of gunpowder on the occupation of the knight. What was the significance of the appearance of Don Quixote? The palace v. the castle. How does the public lighting of a city indicate a great advance in civilization? Luther and Socrates. Observations of an Italian travelling in England in the time of Elizabeth.

E. MODERN EUROPE, 1648–1880.

I. Aa. *General Study on "Old Régime" in Europe; Age of Louis XIV., Frederick the Great, Anne and the Georges, Maria Theresa, Peter the Great.*

A word should be given in explanation of the phrase, "Old Régime"; strictly speaking, the term should be applied to feudal as distinct from constitutional governments; but I have used it as applying to the absolute monarchies and aristocratic societies developed from feudalism, whose power culminated or began to be broken during this period.

The studies, pp. 446, 451, 458, may be summarized as follows: —

GENERAL VIEW OF "OLD RÉGIME," 1648–1789.

Organizations of Period.

Absolute governments in

France ⎱ developed from feudal royalty.
Spain ⎰

Austria ⎫
Sardinia ⎬ developed from feudal imperial "*marches*."[1]
Prussia ⎭

Russia.

Military despotism in England, under constitutional forms, appearing as the

commonwealth, — republican form.
protectorate, — limited autocracy of Cromwell.[2]

---

[1] These imperial marches were geographically so placed as to be involved in all European affairs. Thus, Savoy was always a felt power in all wars involving Italy, Germany, France, and Spain; Brandenburg lay between the Northern and Western groups of European states, while Austria was still the bulwark of Europe against the Turk. The strength of the Empire lay in its separate members, not in its body.

[2] Although in form limited, the powers assumed by Cromwell differed little from those of the monarchs of the "Old Régime"; the source of his power, however, was popular rather than hereditary, and Parliament alone could raise taxes or grant supplies — notable differences.

Constitutional monarchy in England,
> limited or checked by
>> fixed income of the king.
>> parliamentary control of
>>> law.
>>> finance.
>>> army.
>> ministerial responsibility and majority (party) influence.

Republics in
> America, Switzerland.
> England (see military despotism).
> Holland.

Temporary European leagues, for purposes of
> maintaining "Balance of Power."
> securing international justice.
> obtaining favorable commercial terms.

Great Movements of Age.

International and colonial wars,
> caused by [1]
>> ill-defined boundaries.
>> commercial inequalities.
>> disputed successions to various thrones.
>> desires of Lewis XIV. and Frederic the Great for more territory.
>> Turkish invasion.
>> limited harborage and coast-line of the Baltic.
>> "Balance of Power" system.
> waged in the interests of
>> kings and merchants.

---

[1] These causes may be grouped under the two very general heads of "A desire to win, keep, or increase royal power of the feudal type," and "A desire for commercial advantage"; after gaining the points given in the summary, the teacher might set the question, "Reduce these causes to two general statements," as an exercise in generalization. On comparing these causes of war with those of the preceding period, it will at once appear how decidedly men's minds had passed from religious to secular interests. Of course, so far as these wars grew out of desire for territory, they naturally resulted from the feudal organization, which associated dominion with land-ownership.

GENERAL VIEW OF "OLD RÉGIME."— *Continued.*
    resulting in
        development of groups [1] of European lands,—
            Western: Spain, France, England, Netherlands; Germany, Italy, and Austria, involved.
            Northern: Scandinavia, Denmark, northern states of Germany, Russia, Poland.
            South-eastern: Turkey; Austria and Russia involved.
        colonial and commercial annoyance and disturbance.
        devastation of European lands.
        misery of common people through
            disturbance of occupation.
            ruin of land and home.
            military service.
            taxes.
    Revolt, or tendency to revolt, against "Old Régime" in England, America, France.

Relative Strength of European States.
    France strongest in age of Lewis XIV., } as proved by
    Austria second in rank,
        territorial gains; European alliances against them.
    Brandenburg most rapidly growing state, proved by
        value and power in military affairs.
        comparison of territory at beginning and close of period.
    Italy weakest during whole period, proved by her constant territorial loss.
    Poland most rapidly losing power, proved by
        her comparative share in affairs at beginning and end of age.
        her first partition.

---

[1] Note that the leaders of the Western group are the lands of the Rhine and the Atlantic seaboard. The Northern group has the Baltic for its commercial centre, the South-eastern group has the Black Sea, with Constantinople for its Gibraltar. Again, the Western group was bound together by its historic relations with Rome.

MODERN EUROPE. 131

England first commercial and naval power [1] } note treaties and
Holland second commercial and naval power } wars.

Characteristics of Age.
    Absolutism of monarchs, displaying itself in
        disposal [2] of European lands; note the
           "Chambers of Reunion."
           seizure of Strasburg.
           treaties of Utrecht and Rastadt.
           divisions of Italy.
           seizure of Silesia.
           partition of Poland.
        arbitrary [2] declarations of war on their own behalf.
    Decrease of religious intolerance, seen in
        changed causes of wars.
        spirit and material of literature.
    Growth of republican, democratic, revolutionary ideas in literature.
    Growth of positive intellectual interests.
        Natural science, —
           chemistry.
           physics.
           astronomy.   } New.
           botany.
           zoölogy.
        Political economy.
        Philosophy of history and politics (common to England and France).
        Mental and moral philosophy (common to all Europe).
    Development of literature as a political, social, religious, and moral power, seen in
        close relation of English literature, politics, and religion of seventeenth century.

---

[1] The English possession of Gibraltar, giving her the command of the Mediterranean, was one of her most important commercial acquisitions.

[2] These may be regarded as euphemisms for actions which, in private life, and on a petty scale, would be described as dishonest, mean, cruel, or unjust.

GENERAL VIEW OF "OLD RÉGIME." — *Continued.*
        new, popular classes of literature, —
            periodicals.
            novels.
        satirical attacks (note caricature also).
        influence of English politics on French thought.
        censorship of the press.
Foundations for truth, sought in
    nature.
    reason.
    history.
Growth of philanthropic spirit.
General material and intellectual progress, favored by
    royal interest and patronage.
        enormous development of popular literature.
        invention of machinery (*the steam-engine*).
        invention of apparatus.

Nothing more strongly marks the political progress of this age than the drawing together of the states of Europe into a single commonwealth of nations, conscious of mutual relations and interests. This consciousness expressed itself in constant attempts to preserve the "Balance of Power" by temporary alliances against any state which, for the time being, threatened to become too strong for her neighbors, or by such compromises as that by which Poland was first divided between the jealous powers about her.

While a general system of European politics was thus developing, England was leading the way to the modern system of government, that depends for its support on popular suffrage, and organizes itself in representative forms. Even the restored Stuarts belonged rather to the modern than the old *régime*, and from the fall of Charles the First, England could no longer be properly classed as a feudal state, although many feudal forms remained, notably the old assembly of the first estate in the House of Lords. From that time, the House of Commons became the strongest political power in England, although at first it used that power so timidly, that often the king still had his way; but that Parliament was in reality the stronger is proved by the inability of either of the restored Stuarts to carry their measures quite against its will. But with the "Declaration of Rights," Parliament became visibly the chief political power, since it held in its own hands the constant control of the law, of the treasure, of the army. In this expressed change consisted the accomplished "Revolution of 1688," a revolution which the Commons could easily maintain by the absolute dependence of the executive upon them for financial support. Shortly after this revolution, two new features of the constitution became decidedly visible: one, the development of a responsible ministry in sympathy with the majority of the popular vote;[1] the other, the development of rival parties in the country; each party striving to educate public opinion according to its own standards and desires; and each party driving or driven in turn to the various political reforms called for by actual circumstance or by popular theory.

When one notes how all the tendencies, interests, and positive growths of this time are those which are still in our own century, urging their way to culmination, he may perhaps feel justified in including the age in the modern period, in spite of the completed feudal forms it presents in leading states. But the states' system of Europe, the appearance of popular representation in government, of religious toleration,[2] of free speech and popular agitation in regard to the gravest affairs, — of machine work in industry, of the novel and the newspaper in literature, the development of natural science, the growth of philanthropy, — all these things unite the age with ours by close organic ties.

---

[1] But it must be remembered that the "popular vote" of the whole of this period was very limited, according to present standards, and that the House of Commons was essentially aristocratic in composition and feeling.

[2] It must be noted that religious toleration was a tendency rather than a fact. The acts of the first freely elected parliament of the Restoration show how intolerant the majority of the English people still were; while James was driven from the throne quite as much on account of his attitude toward papists, as on account of his arbitrary government.

Subjects for Essay and Examination Work. — The political crimes of the eighteenth century. Was the Navigation Act a permanent advantage to England? (Debate.) Why should the Baltic be a cause of war? The mediæval causes for the weakness of Italy during this age. Views of a peasant in the Palatinate on the policy of Lewis XIV. Views of a French peasant on the same subject. Relation of colonial affairs to international European wars. Review of the growth of Brandenburg into the kingdom of Prussia.[1] Imaginary dialogue between Russia, Prussia, and Austria on the partition of Poland. Value of Constantinople to Russia.

I. Ab. *Special Study of the "Old Régime" in France (Eighteenth Century Type).*

The results of this study may be embodied in some such summary as the following : —

"OLD RÉGIME" IN FRANCE (EIGHTEENTH CENTURY).

Organization, Absolute Feudal Monarchy (compare later Roman Empire and Oriental despotisms).
    Supported by
        the favor of its privileged classes, —
            officers of army and state, ⎫
            the officials of the church, ⎬ opposed to reform.
            an hereditary nobility, ⎭
        the revenue from
            feudal dues.
            arbitrary taxes.
            the sale of offices, privileges, and titles.
            borrowed money.
        a standing army.
    Producing, or marked,
        in administration, by
            confusion.
            injustice and inequality.

---

[1] Similar subjects may be given in connection with the growths of Savoy and Austria.

strong centralization.
corruption and favoritism.
official neglect and idleness.
attempts at reform,[1]
    aiming at
        equality
            of taxation.
            of opportunity.
            before the law.
        religious toleration.
        legal uniformity.
        freedom of trade.
        freedom of thought and speech.
        economy at court.
    failing, through
        selfish interests of privileged classes.
arbitrary laws, taxes, etc.
repression of
    free speech and
    a free press.
neglect of local interests, —
    roads,
    schools,
    churches, etc.
in finance, by
    extravagance, insufficient revenue to meet expenses;[2] ∴.
    debt, dishonesty.
in law, by
    venality (buying and selling of office, and of justice itself).
    unequal punishments, based on class distinction.
    barbarous punishments.
    uncertain, tardy, and varied justice.

---

[1] Compare these attempted reforms with modern ideas, and with the actual changes brought about in France by the Revolutionary period.

[2] This is the prime difficulty which hampers the government, but gives to France her one effective means for forcing reform. (Compare England before the Civil Wars.)

"Old Régime" in France. — *Continued.*
            in the church, by
                    close union of church and state ;
                    intolerance.
                    corruption, simony.
                    inequality, based on class distinctions.
            in the army, by
                    corruption.
                    inequality and injustice (class distinctions).
                    compulsory and oppressive enlistment.
                    no chance for honorable promotion.
            in trade, by
                    government interference.
                    exclusive guild monopoly ; ∴
                            careless work.
                            high prices.
            in society, by
                    hereditary status ; ∴
                    unequal opportunity for
                            official position.
                            acquirement of wealth.
                            acquirement of education.
                    dependence of talent on royal or aristocratic favor.

The Life of France.
    At court,
            marked by
                    extravagance, in behalf of pleasure and pomp.
                    immorality.
                    neglect of state interests.
                    love of pleasure.
            supported by
                    bad debts to the bourgeoisie.
                    oppressive feudal taxation.
            resulting in
                    the formation of corrupt and mischievous ideals, —
                            pleasure.
                            idleness.
                            splendor.
                    careless and mischievous administration.
                    financial embarrassment.

Among the bourgeoisie,
    marked by
        honesty.
        domestic virtue.
        industry and intelligence.
        public interest.
    resulting in
        prosperity and comparative wealth.
        disapproval of the court.
        desire for government reform.[1]
        comparative political importance.
Among the peasants,
    marked by
        extreme poverty.
        extreme physical misery.
        extreme ignorance and superstition.
        oppressive taxation and overwork.
        no protection for property or labor.
        enforced monopolies (*gabelle*, etc.).
    resulting in
        inferior development of French resources,
        blind dissatisfaction and unintelligent revolt,
        development of dangerous classes,
        physical degradation of peasant,
        desire for destruction of "Old Régime."

Thought and Feeling.
    Of the supporters of royalty, —
        belief in divine origin and support of kings; ∴.
        feeling that disloyalty is irreligious.
        belief in arbitrary right of the king
            to change or neglect the law.
            to claim and use the property of the realm.[2]

---

[1] The *bourgeoisie* would try to reform rather than destroy the "Old Régime," since violent change is always opposed to the interests of trade; while to the peasant, revolution could only mean change for the better.

[2] These beliefs in regard to the king had their historic reason. The idea of his "divine right" arose partly from the Scriptural presentation of Hebrew royalty, and partly from the close relations of the heads of church and state during the Middle Ages; his relation to the law as its

"Old Régime" in France. — *Continued.*
        servility and dependence.
        fear of Voltaire, Rousseau, and their followers.[1]
        sentimental sympathy for the poor.[2]
   Of Voltaire, Rousseau, Helvetius, and their followers, —
      revolt against absolutism of king.
      admiration of English thought and government.
      demand for free thought and speech.
      demand for popular power to change laws.
      demand for equality before the law.
      demand for equal education (opportunity).
      belief in common right to the land.
      belief in happiness as standard of morality,
      belief in experience as only source of knowledge,
      loss of any fixed standard of right-doing.

A thorough understanding of the "Old Régime" is essential to a clear understanding of the Revolution, which was by no means a single revolt against a single thing, but a complex turmoil arising from the clash of strong and wealthy classes, of inexperienced thinkers, of ignorant and desperate masses, against an ancient, rigid system, which had spread root and branch through every institution, every industry, every habit of French life. It is therefore necessary to look fairly at this system, and understand just its relations to *each* great class of society, and again, to examine as far as we can into the status of each of these classes, in order that we may understand the elements as well as the causes of the inevitable Revolution.

---

source and chief executive, gave rise to the feeling that he was above the law; while the whole feudal system rested on the theory that all land-titles derived their first validity from royal grants.

[1] No fact more thoroughly proves the influence of Voltaire and Rousseau than this fear practically expressed through a severe censorship of their writings.

[2] That this sympathy was sentimental, was proved fast enough by the strenuous opposition made by the upper classes to the genuinely helpful reforms proposed by Turgot and Necker.

For the Revolution was inevitable; the king could no longer force money from the third estate and the peasantry; long wars, and the fetters imposed on industry by the feudal régime, had exhausted or bound fast the resources of France; and large masses of men, even the king himself, had come face to face with the primal question, "How to live?" Aside from this, men everywhere found themselves hampered and embarrassed, if not absolutely wronged, by an unavoidable subordination to an unwieldy mediæval system. There is no more striking example in all history of the power of an organization to shape the life of men unfortunately than is furnished by this "Old Régime"; the nobles, shut out by law or custom from commercial and professional careers, became a mass of idle, pleasure-loving landlords, dependent on the king for their occupations and honors; the peasants necessarily starved and deteriorated under a system which held them fast to the land, and, at the same time, demanded a disproportionate share of taxes and of heavy physical toil; the bourgeoisie, more healthfully situated, free merchants of the towns or cities, with an assured market, were the soundest men of France,— thoughtful, industrious, and somewhat fitted for citizenship.

Among such materials, the ideas of Voltaire and Rousseau might well be feared by those who wished to uphold the "Old Régime," since in their pages its very foundations were attacked; according to them, the law, the land, the very constitution, were primarily for the good of the people, and should be under their control. That law and government should emanate from popular sources is an idea now considered fundamental, but in the France of the eighteenth century it was revolutionary, although naturally called forth by the abuses of an absolute and arbitrary rule. Rousseau went further, and affirmed that the land should belong to all the people, a demand easy to comprehend when we remember that absolutism had abused its power here also, and had devoted large tracts of French territory to the purposes of idle pleasure, while no hard-working peasant was secure in its use or possession.

Thought was indeed the most dangerous enemy of the "Old Régime"; its financial support, and the mass of its standing army, were drawn from classes that would with reason desire thoroughly to change or destroy it, the instant that their eyes and minds were opened to its injustice, awkwardness, and weakness. The difficulties in their way were meanwhile great, — the powerful landed interests of the clergy and the nobles; their own ignorance or inexperience; the dangers with which revolution always threatens property; the practical hindrances to united action found in bad and uncertain roads, and in the natural inertia of men in regard to great and general affairs. That in spite of all, the Revolution came, proves that France had a vital need for "*Liberty, Equality, Fraternity*"; — for freedom of trade, of thought, of speech; for equality before the law; for equal chances to learn and labor; for a truly sympathetic fraternity between class and class. The whole of continental Europe was full of misery, but France saw light; for in England and America the day had dawned.

Suggestions for Essay and Examination Work. — Stupidities of the "Old Régime." Did they originate in stupidity? Defend your position. Why should the peasants of France become *enraged*, rather than thoughtful, under the "Old Régime"? Account by a common French soldier of his experiences in the army. Reminiscences of an "Invalide." What were the "prospects" open to young Frenchmen of each class during the eighteenth century? Reflections of Necker on the usefulness of a French minister. Why should thoughtful Frenchmen admire England? Why should the ideal prevalent at court not spoil the "Bourgeoisie"? A peasant's notion of reform. A noble's. A merchant's.

E. II. FRENCH REVOLUTION AND WARS OF NAPOLEON, 1789–1815.

Each of the studies, 1, 2, and 3, should be summarized and finished before passing on to new work. The following tabulations may prove helpful: —

1. FRENCH REVOLUTION.

Caused by:

    Arbitrary absolutism of "Old Régime;" ∴
        Oath of Tennis-court.
    A standing army under absolute royal control; ∴
        formation of "National Guard."
    Feudal oppressions of nobles; ∴
        destruction of title-deeds.
    Instability of law and government; ∴
        demand for a signed constitution as a received and understood standard of government.[1]
    Exemption of nobles and clergy from taxation; ∴
        resignation of feudal privilege by the nobles.
        confiscation of church property to state use.
    Degradation and ignorance of lowest classes; ∴
        cruel and unintelligent action in revolution.
    Suppression of free thought and religious intolerance; ∴
        reaction to worship of "Reason."

Favored by:

    Weakness of "Old Régime," seen in
        inability to suppress revolution or preserve order.
        attempted flight of king.
        "emigration" of nobles.
        sudden completeness of its fall.

---

[1] The demands of this first constitution show what wrongs the middle class — the third estate — had most keenly felt; namely, taxation without representation, arbitrary and uncertain law, and the exhaustion of French blood and treasure in foreign wars, waged at the will of the king.

FRENCH REVOLUTION. — *Continued.*

    General French sympathy[1] with the Revolution, strengthened by
        attacks of foreign powers.
        vacillation and weakness of king.

Marked by:
  (1) Rapid succession of constitutional changes.
  (2) Popular suspicions of league of European kings, ∴
        determination to execute Lewis XVI.[2]
        popular energy in foreign wars.
  (3) Despotism under republican forms, Sept., 1792 to July, 1794,
      embodied in
          Parisian clubs and committees.
          demagogic autocrats (Robespierre).
      proving its nature by
          arbitrary imprisonment and massacre.
          "Reign of Terror."
          imposition of revolutionary worships.
      supported by
          terrorism, —
              imprisonment.
              assassination.
              condemnation without trial.
          mob violence.
  (4) Reaction against mob-rule, and gradual restoration of order,
      embodied in
          Directory.
          constitution of year VIII., Napoleonic rule.
      supported by
          national forces, led by
          Napoleon Bonaparte.
  (5) Foreign conquest, accompanied by
  (6) Proclamation of republican principles, and
      Enforcement of republican constitutions in conquered territory.

---

[1] Had the body of the people been attached to the "Old Régime," of course it could not finally have been overthrown, since perhaps even the peasants would have made a good defence, judging from their energy in the Vendéan War.

[2] The whole government of the "Old Régime" had been so absolutely centralized in the person of the monarch, that to the peasants and the populace, at least, the execution of the king would mean the fall of the whole system.

Results of Revolution.
    Military autocracy of Napoleon.[1]
    Uniform system of published law (Code Napoleon).
    A published constitution, open to popular criticism.
    Established recognition of the representative principle.
    Destruction of feudalism; ∴
        equality before the law.
        uniform system of taxation substituted for feudal dues.
    Formation of a national army.
    Development of French patriotism, through
        common sufferings and achievements.
        foreign attack, and
        Napoleon's victories.

Although the "Old Régime" apparently fell at a blow before the first attack of vigorous revolution, we must still remember with Taine, that its spiritual forces, its habits of thought and action, were powerful factors throughout the Revolutionary age; perhaps indeed they still possess a governing force in France. America was too recent and distant an experiment to have any practical lessons to teach, while English kings still managed by various forms of bribery and trickery to govern more in sympathy with the old than with the coming political system of Europe. France herself only knew by experience one way of government, the way of centralized despotism, and throughout her attempts at political liberty, this political habit clung. The most ardent defenders of the "Rights of Man," when they obtained the power and responsibility of government, could not see their way clear to solve the problem of securing order at home and victory abroad, without recourse to force, and the representative machine was far too imperfect and ill-adjusted to work out desirable results, especially in a period so full of rapid and critical dangers. Taine has clearly shown that the despotisms of the "Old Régime" were to blame for the despotisms of the Revolution; but perhaps he does not. suffi-

---

[1] The comparison between Cromwell and Napoleon is a natural and striking one; but it applies rather to their circumstances than their characters.

ciently emphasize the "*dire necessity,*" which day after day forced on bold but inexperienced men to some sort of great and decisive action, involving the movements of troops, the wholesale judgments of courts, the suppression of disturbance, the defence of legislative bodies, the conclusion of treaties. Even a modern state, with a smoothly working representative system, with railway and telegraph and newspaper at command, in such a time of foreign and domestic stress, would find itself urged to some form of easily and rapidly acting autocracy. It is beyond all doubt that France could not change in less than a generation, if, indeed, so quickly, from the "Old Régime" to a genuine republic of any sort. How badly even the most advanced republicans understood the spirit they had evoked was shown by the enforcement of republican forms and names upon countries prepared neither to understand nor be grateful for them. Under these conditions, it was fortunate for France that the Directory, driven for self-preservation to the protection of Napoleon, found in him a master for itself and France; a master of sufficient genius to hold France firm to the acknowledged principles of the Revolution; a master who knew how to give France law and order and peace under the new forms which she herself could not yet use; and a master representative in his own person of popular government.

The constitution of the year VIII. differed vastly from the "Old Régime," in that it recognized the people as a part of the government of France, and brought the whole country under a uniform standard of law. Although in France, as in England, revolution did not at once change the *reality* of various political relations, yet it gave men new forms and new tools, better fitted to the spirit and tendency of the age. Little by little the new forms were to become inspired with the breath of popular life, and little by little the new tools were to gain edge and temper and strength, as the awkward grasp of the people became surer and finer.

The Revolution is even more striking from the social than the political standpoint; and its political results may almost be regarded as a necessary outcome of its social changes. Its essential fact was, that it overthrew feudalism, or a society based on hereditary status, and gave to France instead a nation of citizens and a society based upon equal relationship to a common soil.

2. THE NAPOLEONIC RULE.

Developed by:
    Necessities of France for
        domestic peace.
        foreign victory.
    Military genius of Napoleon.

Supported by:
    Patriotism of France, and
    Loyalty of armies to Napoleon.
    Napoleonic recognition of republican principles and forms.[1]

Resulting in:
    Recovery of Rhine frontier for France. (Compare with boundary of ancient Gaul.)
    Growth of Napoleonic Empire. (Compare with Empire of Charlemagne.)
    Fall of "Holy Roman Empire." [2]
    European opposition to Napoleon[3] and revolutionary principles, caused by
        fear of his military genius.

---

[1] Note Napoleon's recognition of the principle of manhood suffrage in his own elevation; but in his arbitrary disposal of the various parts of his empire, he followed the spirit and example of the "Old Régime."

[2] In order to call attention to this rather uninfluential event, the teacher should remind the class that it was the title of Augustus Cæsar, which came to its end in 1806; and that from this Holy Roman Empire have been formed Italy, Germany, Austria, Poland, Holland, Belgium, and Switzerland.

[3] It is interesting to note how neighborly jealousies sometimes overcame the common fear of Napoleon, as when Austria and Prussia joined him against Russia. In the early part of the Revolution, also, France was often indebted to various European jealousies or rival ambitions.

The Napoleonic Rule. — *Continued.*
        spread of the republican principles which he claimed to personify.[1]
        fall of Napoleon.
        national reactions against foreign influence or rule, in
            Spain.
            Russia.
            Prussia.
    resulting in
        readjustment of Europe at Congress of Vienna.

The Congress of Vienna proved itself the representative of the "Old Régime," not only by its restorations of old dynasties, but by its arbitrary disposal of European lands and peoples.

3. PRUSSIAN REVOLUTION.

Developed by:
    Necessity of Prussia for
        forces
        funds   } to cope with Napoleon.
        patriotism
    Failure of "Old Régime" to meet this necessity, because of
        inequality and inadequacy of taxation.
        entire separation of people and government.
        fixed nature of occupations;[2] ∴
        loss of free energy.
        fixed tenure and status of land; ∴
        inadequate development of Prussian resources.
        popular sympathy with French Revolution.
    Genius of Stein and his associates.

---

[1] The formation of the "Holy Alliance" proves how thoroughly the monarchs of Europe realized that Napoleon was not their final foe, but rather the ideas which he had nominally represented.

[2] For the historic origin of the three classes of Prussia, with their corresponding occupations, see "Studies," p. 226.

Resulting in
    Formation of a national army, ⎫
    Abolition of serfdom,   ⎪ Reforms of Stein, Scharn-
    Free trade in land,   ⎬ horst, and their associ-
    Free choice of occupation to Prus- ⎪ ates. Compare with
        sian citizens;   ⎭ Turgot.
    Nationalization of Prussia; ∴
    Growth of patriotism, developed by
        reform of the state.
        example of Spain.[1]
        agitation of secret societies.
        active efforts of enthusiastic patriots, —
            Arndt, poet.
            Jahn, gymnast.[2]
            Fichte, philosopher.
        statesmanship of Stein.
    War of Liberation.
    Recognition of constitutional principles.[3]

The French and the Prussian Revolutions were caused by similar needs, and effected similar ends; both were forced on by the demand of the government for money, which an exhausted land could by no means yield, and for popular sympathies, which an oppressed peasantry and a neglected middle class could by no means give; and both ended in most radical change, — in the destruction of the rigid feudal state, with its classes, lands, and occupations, fixed by distinctions of birth, and in

---

[1] From the extract given on p. 488, it will be seen that the national movement in Spain was greatly intensified by a spirit of religious zeal against the "heretic."

[2] Although there is a touch of romance about the attractive figure of Jahn, his idea was nevertheless far more practical than one at first might think; the splendidly trained peoples of antiquity show what the physical culture of the individual may accomplish for the race; while in the Prussian army we have the modern application of the same principle.

[3] These, however, did not begin to work so quickly in Germany as in France; but the seed was planted; and its life was in it, "after its kind," from the day that Stein called together again the old mediæval estates, which were in their spirit and origin popular assemblies.

the erection instead of the mobile modern state, with its free citizens, lands, and trades. But while the French Revolution was precipitated upon an unprepared, inert, and helpless government which must needs fall before its onset, the Prussian Revolution was the result of strong and simple statesmanship, whose measures were carried out by government itself, and carried out so peacefully that men were scarcely aware that Prussia as well as France and England had entered the world of modern states. The revolution was the less marked because the fundamental change was social, as in France; and here it was unaccompanied by any agitation for those political changes with which France had terrified Europe. For the time being, Prussia felt no need of such political change. The Prussian monarchs had attended to the duties of their office and the interests of their people far better than the kings of France; the changes of Stein and his associates met the need of the hour; the freeing of serfs and the reform of the army gave Prussia at once a free citizen army, enlivened throughout by the breath of hopeful emulation; free trade in land rendered every acre available to capital; and free choice of occupation allowed every man to serve the state according to his best or favorite capacity; thus the Prussian resources began to gather force and volume from farm and shop and counter; and the free citizens became better and better able to bear the burdens of taxation. Meanwhile, all these reforms made Prussia a country to be loved, so that the revolution at home, and admiration for Stein, began to neutralize the effects of the Revolution in France and admiration for Napoleon.

From the day that Stein noticed the power of the Spanish revolt, he regarded the passion of patriotism, the sentiment of nationality, as the mightiest foe that could be evoked against Napoleon; hence his eagerness to spread the news of it, and to rouse the national pride to enthusiasm by poetry and stirring example. That Napoleon entirely agreed with Stein's opinion, is easily inferred from his demand for Stein's dismissal; that Stein was wholly right was proved by the event. Even in Yorck, the brave old general, the love of his land overcame his life-long habit of military obedience.

I cannot forbear adding that the development of Prussian nationality is a most significant lesson as to the wide popular effects which the conscious purpose and action of a few united and devoted patriots may achieve.

Suggestions for Essay and Examination Work. — Does the Revolution show the French people to have been eager or slow in regard to political change? Why is a "national guard" the most effective national defence, other things being equal? How did it happen that France, during the Revolutionary period, was so well able to meet foreign invasion? How was the "Old Régime" to blame for the excesses of the Revolution? The inconsistencies of Robespierre. Journal of an "Emigrant." Letters of a Norman noble, present in the national assembly from its opening to Aug. 5, 1789. Letters of a Lyons merchant present during the same period. Mob-rule v. the "Old Régime." Reflections of a Roman citizen on the French proclamation of a Roman republic. Same of a Venetian aristocrat on the proclamation of a Venetian republic. What are the uses of a written constitution?

The working of the "Balance of Power" system during the Napoleonic era. Napoleon and Charlemagne. What popular ideals and desires did Napoleon personify or accomplish? What old historic idea appears in the phrase "Holy Alliance"? How far have the arrangements of the Congress of Vienna remained permanent?

What does the history of the Prussian Revolution show as to the value of personal effort for a great political object? What would have been the opinion of practical, common-sense men as to the advisability of Prussia's making any attempt to resist Napoleon after the Treaty of Tilsit? How did the reforms of Stein increase happiness? Energy? Napoleon v. Stein. Value of secret societies as instruments of agitation. (Debate.)

E. III. THE NINETEENTH CENTURY.

On page 491, a blank space is left after "chief contemporary and original sources," in order that the teacher may have an opportunity to test the pupil's power to recognize the true sources of historical knowledge when he sees them. If he has noted these sources as they have been indicated throughout the work, he will now be ready to see that the contemporary world is full of the original "raw material" of nineteenth century history; that it is appearing in newspapers, in new laws, in contemporary literature and art, in declarations of war and treaties of peace, in statistics, in investigations and inventions, in amusements and manners; and, above all, in the organizations into which men are crowding the forces of numbers and knowledge, or from which they are silently withdrawing these forces. If the class be sufficiently mature, there is no better place than this to enter upon some discussion of the comparative value of historic materials, and to note the tests by which this or that should be rejected as useless. But even with the most mature pupils that are likely to use this book, it may not be well to enter further into the matter than to note, that in all the mass of actions, facts, opinions, and objects, which enter into the lives of men, some enter so widely into the lives of the *generality* so as to become positive forms or forces in society, and so rise to be of general typical historic value; and while the student should respect every action, fact, opinion, and object as significant, he should be led to feel a sense of proportion in regard to their relative value.

The "Studies" on 1 and 2 may be summarized somewhat as follows:—

NINETEENTH CENTURY.

Political Organizations.

Constitutional governments, { monarchical (England).
republican (America, France).
imperial (Germany).
    composed of
        an executive head, —
            non-representative and irresponsible (*Ex.:* English monarch).
            representative and responsible (*Exs.:* prime minister, president).
        legislative chambers, —
            upper house:
                hereditary, elected, or appointed.
            lower house:
                elected, more popular than upper.
        courts of justice.
        a democratic body of citizens, bound together by common interests in
            government.
            law.
            defence and commerce.
            education.
            religion.
        common residence on national soil.
    based upon popular approval.
    characterized by
        majority rule.
        universal suffrage, or strong tendency toward it.
        systems of checks.
        legal and political equality of citizens.
        publicity of measures.
        representative system, applied to
            magistrates (*Ex.:* English premier).
            assemblies (*Ex.:* Reichstag).
        citizen-armies.
    aided or rendered possible by
        railroads, telegraphs, steamships, etc.
        newspapers, public education.
        public spirit and interest of citizens.

NINETEENTH CENTURY. — *Continued.*
 The nation-state, bound together by ties of
  common race and speech.
  common religion.
  common government and interests.
   Exs.: Italy, Germany, France, Russia.
 Imperial, colonial union (England),
  composed of
   Europeans, and
   undeveloped or native races.
  developed through
   commercial interests.
   modern means of communication.
 European congresses, conferences, etc.,
  tending to
   unify Europe.
   substitute arbitration for war.
   protect weak states.
   preserve the "Balance of Power."
 Political parties, embodying
  public opinion in working organizations of citizens.
 Secret societies,
  agitating for
   national independence (Germany, Italy, Greece).
   changes in government, —
    constitutional (Germany, Italy).
    communistic or socialistic (France, Germany).
    anarchic (Russia).

Other Organizations.
 The free church in the free state (America).
 Combinations of labor, —
  trades-unions.
  secret societies.
  international unions.
  co-operative unions (*Ex.:* building associations).
  political parties (German socialists).
 Public schools.
 Citizen-armies.

Voluntary societies for
  management of charities.
  agitation of reforms.
  pursuit of learning, etc., etc.
Great corporations for carrying on business enterprises (banking, manufacturing, transportation, telegraphy, etc., etc.).

Great Movements and Tendencies of Age.

Europeanization of other continents,
  { Asia (England, Russia).
  { Africa (England, France).
  { Australia (England).
  in interests of
    commerce.
    Christianity.
Development of nationalities,
  completed in
    Germany, Italy,
    Greece, Holland, Belgium.
  agitated for in
    Hungary, Poland, Ireland.
  proceeding in
    America.
Formation of popular constitutional governments in
  France, Germany, Italy,
  Austria, Spain, etc.
European wars,[1]
  in behalf of
    nationality.
    "Balance of Power."
    colonial interests.
  resulting in
    formation of national units.
    constant checking of greater powers.[2]
    arbitrary disposal of weaker peoples (in some cases).

---

[1] Perhaps no one war outranks in importance the Franco-Prussian, which at one blow made France a republic, completed the independence and freedom of Italy, and bound the states of Germany into imperial union.

[2] Notably Russia; on whom Europe has long kept constant watch.

NINETEENTH CENTURY. — *Continued.*

Abolition of slavery and serfdom (England,[1] Russia, Prussia, America).

Socialism,

embodied in

political parties.
secret societies.

aiming at [2]

state ownership of means of labor.
more equitable distribution of profits of labor.
greater leisure and culture for laboring classes.
reorganization of states in the interests of labor.

Characteristics of Age.

Democracy.
Individual freedom of

occupation, labor, movement.
residence.
speech and thought.

Appearance of lowest classes as

members of society (through abolition of slavery and serfdom).
members of the state (through universal suffrage, citizen-armies, and public schools).

Industrial development,

favored by

new means of transportation and communication (railway, telegraph, steamship).
introduction of machinery.
opening of Oriental markets.
development of new lands.

Scientific investigation.
General diffusion of intelligence, comfort, and freedom.

---

[1] In England the slave-owners were paid for their property by the state; in America, through the pressure of circumstance, this property was regarded as "contraband of war."

[2] I have purposely stated these aims in the most general terms, since the name of socialist covers so many theories and desires. A more definite list might be made for class-work by paraphrasing the demands made on pp. 537, 538.

Strained relations of church and state.
Religious toleration, seen in
    Christian and Mohammedan equality in Turkey.
    repeal of corporation and test acts in England.
    Catholic relief act in England.
    disestablishment of Irish " church."
Cosmopolitanism, or diffusion of common thought and knowledge of agricultural, commercial, and mechanical resources.
Increasing number and power of social organizations.

The British constitution is a government machine worked by the people. The powers of the monarch are so hedged about by those of the premier and the commons, the premier is so dependent on the following of the commons, the latter are so readily displaced by the popular vote, and this again is so easily led by argument or personal influence, that no part of the government can long act in a way which people in general regard as foolish or wicked without experiencing a change of heart or a fall. Although in its essential spirit democratic, yet the British constitution is more picturesque than the plainer and severer forms of France and America, since its legislative assemblies find their title and origin in the mediæval assemblies of estates, while the monarch and the court preserve the memories of the "Old Régime." Of these historic forms, the House of Lords and the king appear unnecessary to an American eye, since the real work of government is carried on by the more distinctly modern and representative parts of the constitution, the prime minister and the House of Commons. Although the House of Commons is a representative body in theory, and largely so in fact, it can never be the thorough tool of the democracy until its members are paid for their services, thus allowing the trading and laboring classes to send personal representatives. This imperfection, however, is partly counterbalanced by the superior independence of men, whose living does not depend on their expressed political opinions. The central figure of the government is, of course, the prime minister; he embodies popular will and trust; he is the responsible executive of the nation; and so thoroughly is his power felt to be the leading one, that in common speech the prime minister and his followers are called "the government."

Nothing more strikingly illustrates the great change that has passed over France within the century than to compare her present constitution with that of the "Old Régime"; hereditary distinctions in society have vanished; the whole people share in the government; the church has ceased to be a distinctive part of the state. France indeed has become a more thoroughly modern state than her leader, England, since every part of her government is directly representative of the will of the majority of her citizens, and since her citizens include all eligible Frenchmen at home, or in the colonies. By this last inclusion, France has succeeded in binding her colonies to herself in organic union, and thus in forming a genuine "Greater France."

Germany differs from England and France in that it is a complex of historic states, where the problem of representation has been more difficult, because not only citizens but governments must be represented. These governments, too, differ widely in spirit, form, history, and power; while one of them, the Prussian, maintains among the others a leadership almost amounting to autocracy. But the elastic fitness of the English constitution to modern political needs receives no better illustration than the fact that it has been made the successful working basis for the governments of two states so widely different as Germany and France, — the former the home of particularism, the latter thoroughly stamped with centralization.

Not only the principles but the forms of these modern constitutions run parallel. To the king corresponds the emperor and the president; the latter, however, adds to his power the responsibility of a prime minister. This responsibility and a limited term of office give him checks felt neither by king nor emperor. With the premier ranks the chancellor; the House of Lords is copied by the French Senate and the German Bundesrath; while the purely nineteenth century parts of the constitution, the lower houses and the citizen body, are very nearly alike.

The modern state thus stands before us, the complete, adjustable organ of popular will. It has secured itself against domestic tyranny by a cunning system of constant and balanced checks; against foreign invasion by citizen-armies and a central responsible chief. It embodies within itself the representative principle discovered by the towns in the feudal age, and the equal citizenship of the classic republics; but it has learned to combine the two, so that its popular assemblies are neither confined to the representation of a single city as in antiquity, nor to the representation of separate hereditary classes as in the mediæval age. The newspaper and the telegraph serve the purpose of the crowded "market-place," and enable a widely scattered population to learn, discuss, and judge at the same hour the events of each passing day, thus binding areas of thousands of miles into an intelligent, sympathetic, political unit. Thus for the state, space is destroyed; and the practical difficulty felt by antiquity of forming a successful republic larger than the area of a single city, has disappeared. Nevertheless, in the modern as in the ancient state, "Persuasion" is the goddess who grants political power; a power no man can keep unless he keep as well the approval of the majority of his fellow-citizens. Our armies, again, are of a new type. The mercenaries who played so important a part in antiquity, the mediæval warrior-bands of vassals, following their knightly landlords, are alike displaced by citizen-armies, regularly trained and paid to serve their *whole* country and their *own* country.

In noting the other features of organized social life in our own century, we are struck by the endless number of organizations, and by the fact that they are almost without exception formed in the interests of genuine progress, and that a progress toward the higher, freer, more spiritual life of man. Many of them are absolutely new; others bear some resemblance to older forms; thus, the trades-union recalls the guild, the colonial empire of England has points of resemblance with the empire of Rome. But the resemblances are superficial; the time is great and original, and gives its own peculiar stamp to all its living forms.

The constitutional state is distinctly of the nineteenth century; the nation-states appeared with the opening of the Renaissance, but our own century has notably increased their number, strengthened the spirit of nationality and the consciousness of race-relationships. Thus in the modern as the ancient state appears the strong kinship bond with a common fatherland or mother-country as a common ancestor. The strong tendency toward the formation of these national units is seen in the almost constant agitation, which desires for nationalization have produced in one or another part of Europe. This desire has divided the Holy Roman Empire since its final fall into its true component parts, — a Protestant, Dutch-speaking Holland; a Catholic, French-speaking Belgium; a Catholic Italy; a union of the old German-born and German-speaking tribes into a Teutonic empire; with this desire, Hungary has disturbed Austria; Ireland besieged England; Poland roused the sympathies and sometimes the indignation of civilized states; pleading the rights of nationality, Greece commanded the services of Europe to obtain them; by national sympathies or aspirations, Turkey has lost wholly, or in part, one after another of her little Slavic and Christian principalities, until, dismembered and disjointed, the Moslem Oriental state has won the nickname of the "Sick Man" of Europe.

How far nationality can really settle the independence and the boundaries of European states is still an open question. When political boundaries follow strongly marked geographical barriers, such as Italy, Spain, and England possess, we will hardly expect political disturbance arising from this source; but the partition of Poland shows how helpless a country is without such natural defences, while the able and increasingly successful agitations, for "Home-Rule" in Hungary and Ireland, have been strongly backed by their real geographical unity. Germany, however, lies between two badly defined boundaries; and the shifting fortunes of her Russian and French frontiers have proved already, and may perhaps in future prove, a source of serious difficulty with a greedy or discontented neighbor.

While Europe thus individualizes within, a glance at the map (pp. 520, 521) will show how rapidly she is penetrating or possessing the rest of the world. Since the opening of the sixteenth century, the great movement of population has been from Europe outward; her peoples have "swarmed" westward, eastward, southward; with them they have carried their material civilization, their ideas, their institutions; already the world itself grows cosmopolitan; and each land gives of its own good in return for that of every other. As the Greek peopled the Ægæan coasts and islands, as the Macedonian hellenized Western Asia, as the Roman peopled and civilized the lands of the Mediterranean basin, so the European will possess the world. With each of these movements, civilization has swept through wider circles of land and population; on comparing its present area with that which it held a thousand years B.C., we note a marvellous change; then, in a little knot of Oriental states, a rich, material civilization concentrated its enjoyments and powers in the lives of nobles, kings, priests, and merchants; now three great continents are thoroughly possessed by free peoples, among whom a high type of material and intellectual civilization is widely spread, and still more widely spreading; and the same leaven has begun to work through the continents that remain.

But the movement is not all peaceful; the urgent Europeans threaten to crowd each other hard in the most desirable parts of the outlying world; in fact, the international relations of Europe are largely determined by colonial and commercial considerations; thus Russia and England threaten in Asia, and clashing colonial interests may mean European war; thus the determination that Russia shall not win Constantinople, prolongs the existence of Turkey, and decides the combinations of Europe in every Eastern complication.

Turning from the general history of Europe to the history of special countries, we find in nearly every case that this is so entangled with international or cosmopolitan movements that it only gives particular illustrations of general historic tendencies. Thus in England, as everywhere, the advance of democracy, colonial and commercial interests, and the problems of labor, have been the centres of action. There, as elsewhere, democracy has grown more and more complete with the advancing century; one has but to compare the demands of the Chartists with the reforms made by Parliament from 1848 onward, to see how rapidly this political tendency has changed from the dread to the pet of the public; those demands, so shocking to the English feeling of the former time, are now almost wholly answered. There, as elsewhere, but more than elsewhere, commerce has led men forth to civilize and conquer. So important are her colonies and her commercial routes, that the foreign relations of England may almost be explained by reference to these alone. Thus the fear of Russia determines her attitude in all affairs where Constantinople is threatened or involved, while the Suez Canal, her all-important highway to India, constantly entangles her in Egyptian affairs. In her colonial and commercial relations, England has proven herself at times the benefactor, at times the oppressor, of inferior races. But it may perhaps be said that such acts of injustice as the Opium War, and the imposition of her own ruler in Afghanistan, have been overbalanced by the higher civilization she has introduced, by the roads she has opened, by the missionaries and schools she has protected, and by such measures as the abolition of widow-burning and the suppression of the Thugs in India.

In England, too, as elsewhere, the problems of labor have caused threatening movements and important legislation. First, the progress of mechanical invention substituted machines for men in manufactures; the first result of this was to throw out of work a mass of artisans, mostly skilled laborers, who had no other way of making a living than that the machine had taken. Then came the Corn-laws, which injured all classes by raising the price of bread, and only benefited for the time being the English wheat-growers, who, by holding a monopoly of a prime necessity, could say to the public, "Your money or your life." All along, too, one serious element[1] in the Irish problem has been a labor-question in regard to the due relations of various classes to the soil.

In France, again, the trends of the century appear. The restored Bourbons, though forced to recognize constitutional forms, did not even learn from the Revolution that peace and order lay in the development, not the suppression, of liberty, and came back rather with memories of "how they used to do" than ideas of "how they ought to do." Their measures against the freedom of the press, as well as those taken afterwards by the third Napoleon, show how thoroughly men have begun to realize that the printing-press is the most formidable of modern political forces, since it is our present "organ of persuasion." That Louis Napoleon, although following much in their footsteps, did not follow the Bourbons into banishment, was due to the power of his name, which was associated with an epoch of true *national* glory, and with the first days of peaceful freedom from the "Old Régime." By appealing, too, to the universal vote, he not only recognized the fundamental political change of the Revolution,[2] but assured his election by throwing it into the hands of an ignorant majority, whose political education had not yet extended far enough thoroughly to comprehend the Napoleons, beyond their "outward show."

---

[1] This is a social element; added to this, as a political grievance, has been the lack of "Home-rule." (See also p. 159 of this manual, and compare Hungary.)

[2] The political revolution of modern times seems to be as thoroughly established in France as in England; but France is as seriously threatened as the rest of the world by the social revolution springing from the demands of labor, and in Germany the story is the same.

The special studies on the German Empire and the kingdom of Italy not only show the development of two powerful modern states, but also illustrate the conquering power of ideas and ideals when once they reach the popular masses. In both countries the leading movements have been the same, — towards national union, and towards constitutional liberty; of these, the latter has been part of an impulse common to all the civilized peoples of our century; the former has been distinctive of Germany and Italy, among the greater powers.

In Germany, as in France, the free press has been the terror of the "Old Régime," and for the same reasons; but in Germany has been added to that the influence of the schools and universities; the censorship of the press and that of the university have been the new persecutions which these new weapons have evolved; although Austria has endeavored to meet them by set teaching of the principles and spirit of the older order. When Frederick William the Fourth declares, "A sheet of paper shall not come between me and my subjects," he forgets that, in the large modern state, a sheet of paper is the only possible means of communication between a monarch and his busy, widely-scattered subjects.

But the outcome of events in Germany proves, beyond a doubt, the use of long-continued political agitation as an agent of political change. In Germany, as elsewhere, it has led to the full recognition of the principle that government should be for the people and by the people. The development of German unity shows the value of still another power in politics, — the power of enthusiasm. The common forms and traditions, the heroes and the deeds that warmed men's hearts with common pride in the German name, roused that pride at length to the making of an empire and a nation.

The latest history of Italy, even more than that of Germany, has an epic unity and spirit. In 1815 Savoy alone was under native rule; her government alone could appeal to native support and sympathy. As part of the Holy Roman Empire,

Italy had become since the days of Charles the Fifth, partly heritage of Spain, and partly heritage of Austria, while in the days of Pepin and Charlemagne, the pope had received as a gift his part of the soil of the Christian Empire.

In Italy, the movement for nationality, inspired by the love of independence, — and the movement for constitutionalism, inspired by the love of political liberty, were each sustained by great historic memories, reaching back to the days of the later Roman republic, when Italy was free, united, and great.

Although the interference of European monarchs in Neapolitan affairs called forth Italian indignation, still it was a pure measure of self-defence, since the stirring of one people against a king might mean the stirring of Europe against the whole monarchic system; thus England had stirred France, — France, Spain and Germany, — and Spain, in turn, had now roused Naples. Naples, indeed, could have been appeased, and the power of the king established by the prudent and genuine grant of a liberal constitution; but with the troops of Austria and the sympathies of the monarchs behind him, the Neapolitan ruler naturally underrated the moral forces springing to arms against him. Indeed, the Italian struggle against Austria was throughout the struggle of moral with physical powers. On the side of Austria were troops, and treasure, and the might of an old, successful name; on the side of Italy were justice, truth, a never-yielding purpose and enthusiasm.

Savoy alone was free to embody and lead the Italian aspirations, and give them political and military force. Victor Emmanuel as the one Italian, the one constitutional ruler of Italy, could command the respect, the loyalty, the admiration, of the whole peninsula. In order that Italy might win attention and respect from the European commonwealth, Cavour involved her in the Crimean War; in order that she might claim the sympathy and aid of France, he gave a daughter of old Savoy in marriage to a Napoleonic adventurer, thus taking advantage, too, of the historic enmity of Austria and France.

The principle of popular government has never been more

absolutely respected nor more nobly used than in uniting state after state to patriotic, liberal Savoy; and never has history more nearly touched the highest poetic justice than in the return of a pure Italian government to Rome, at once the geographic and historic centre of the whole peninsula.

The question is often asked, "What is the relation of biography to history?" In general, it may be said that there are no more important or significant historical facts, and no stronger historical forces, than the lives of men. Wherever the teacher's time is short, and the era he deals with great, he can do no better than to take some one man whose life was thoroughly mingled with that of his time, and make as exhaustive a study as possible of his character, and its relations to the contemporary world. These character-studies form with younger classes an excellent concrete introduction to more abstract historical inquiries; and even in the most abstract of these inquiries, one meets here and there men so intimately connected with affairs, that they seem, as it were, to have embodied their age or country in their own strong personalities. Victor Emmanuel belongs beyond a doubt among such men as these; and Cavour and Mazzini do not fall far short of it. I have, therefore, in p. 533, introduced character-studies of these three, not alone on account of their intrinsic importance, but as excellent examples of the way in which biography and history mingle.

Cavour represents the conservative liberal; the man who neither breaks with the old, nor rejects the new; a man who is at once a devoted patriot and a prudent statesman; a thinker, a worker, but in every deed and thought, practical; with that rare power which can devote itself to an unattained ideal, and at the same time can see the very next step which must be taken to reach it. His patriotism bound him at once to the people and the monarch; his prudence commanded the respect of the most conservative courts, and tempered the ardent action of the king; while that genius of practical imagination which saw the possible relations of the distant and the near, enabled him to turn every circumstance and every resource to the freedom and unity of Italy. To accomplish this, he aimed at two things: to make Piedmont the leader of the peninsula; to bring Italy into the European commonwealth; while besides these immediate objects, his policy always had in mind that "inevitable future" of democracy.

What Cavour would and did accomplish by a policy of compromise and delay, Mazzini wished to do by outspoken war on what he hated, and devotion unto death to what he loved. Each nature had its value in the making of Italy; she needed the utter abandonment of self, the clear vision of ultimate destiny, the religious fervor of Mazzini; perhaps she needed even more the cool head of Cavour, since her foes were more easily to be overcome by skilful diplomacy and prudent delay than by the most ardent essay of arms or eloquence.[1]

Although patriotism was the ruling passion in Cavour and Victor Emmanuel, as well as in Mazzini, in Mazzini this passion became a religion, with Italy for its deity and its conscience; "the martyrs" of the people's cause, "the adoration of principles," "the omnipotent duty," "your country, a visible evangel of love," — these are the phrases of a worship, a faith.

If Cavour was the statesman, and Mazzini the prophet of the Italian movement, Victor Emmanuel was its hero; trained as a soldier, he was bred for a time of war; reared simply and hardily, he had the respect of the simple and hardy classes, and could sympathize with them; trained in the catechism and Roman history, he was a good Catholic and an intelligent patriot; while he had at command the historic and popular tongues of his own Italy, and the cosmopolitan French of his best neighbor. Not only by training, but by nature, he was the true king of Italy; an ardent patriot, he loved his land and

---

[1] The fact that Mazzini was forced to publish his writings in London, shows that the censorship of the press excluded his influence from Italy as much as possible, where he most desired it to be felt; incidentally, too, it shows the political freedom existing in England.

trusted his folk; a prudent liberal, he neither offended too far the European monarchs when he had not power to withstand them, nor did he hold back freedom from the people for an instant after he felt he could defend it; but the man was more than the soldier or statesman; his devoted, self-forgetful enthusiasm drew to him the hearts of the whole people with a tide of passionate loyalty that swept away every barrier that party, and history, and religion itself could rear.

I have named the sketchy extracts, pp. 534–538, a study on socialism, merely for the sake of uniformity, although they are worth little more than to attract attention to the aims of the great social revolution which seems to press nearer and nearer. Perhaps there is no subject of more immediate importance than this, and none more variously understood. The movement in general insists upon a substitution of the co-operative principle for that of competition, and therefore threatens the whole present system of industry; it would make the state the owner of the means of labor, and therefore threatens all private property at present invested in these means with a transfer, if not with a loss; its advocates are inspired with an earnest enthusiasm, and not rarely with a genuine devotion, which gives to socialism the power of a faith; its demands are backed by the actual physical force of an army of laborers, on whom society depends for food, and dress, and shelter, for transportation and protection; in common with Christianity, it teaches the brotherhood of man, and asserts the principle of helpful, social union, as against the law of the "struggle for existence." After noting these points, the teacher may act his own judgment as to how far he may wisely pursue a study, materials for which he will find ready to his hand in every week's news, and in any population among which he lives.

The points to be made from the "Study on 6," p. 539, are for the most part embodied in the foregoing summary. At least two days should be devoted to this study, the second of which may be profitably spent in a general conversation in regard to the points suggested by the questions. The aim of the teacher in this study should be to rouse the student's interest in the greatness of the movements in the midst of which he himself lives.

If the studies from p. 3 to p. 539 have been of any value, the "General Review Study" on the last page needs no comment.

AIDS

FOR

TEACHING GENERAL HISTORY;

INCLUDING

A LIST OF BOOKS RECOMMENDED FOR A
WORKING SCHOOL LIBRARY.

BY

MARY D. SHELDON,

Formerly Professor of History in Wellesley College,
Teacher of History in the Oswego Normal
School, New York, and Author of
Studies in General History.

PUBLISHED BY D. C. HEATH & CO.,
Boston, New York, and Chicago.

1894.

Copyright, 1888,
BY MARY SHELDON-BARNES.

TYPOGRAPHY BY J. S. CUSHING & CO., BOSTON.

AIDS FOR TEACHING GENERAL HISTORY.

THE time has come when the teacher of history, as well as the teacher of chemistry or biology, demands for his work a certain material equipment, which shall enable his pupils to realize some of that mental vigor which springs from individual work with the sources of knowledge. In Germany, this demand has been met by what are known as *Quellenbücher*, or collections of illustrative and original sources; and in my own *Studies in General History*, I have made some attempt to meet such a need for our secondary schools; but even had the teacher some ideal Quellenbuch to place in the hands of his pupils, he would still find that every extension of equipment which can give *new material for work and thought* will pay for itself again and again in results more genuine and lasting.

For the teacher of history, a material equipment mostly consists of pictures, maps, and books. Of pictures, the most valuable are photographs of buildings, statues, monuments, reliefs, and remains in general,[1] — and contemporary prints, portraits, or engravings of the time to be considered. The latter can often be found in desirable reproductions, and teacher and pupil alike will find a great interest in collecting historical cuts and engravings from old and new magazines and the better class of illustrated papers. These, as well as the photographs, should be nicely mounted on separate sheets of uniform style and size, and clearly labelled; in the case of an

---

[1] The Soule Photo. Co., 338 Washington St., Boston, Mass., will furnish on application catalogues of such photographs, *unmounted*, from which a very desirable selection may be made.

engraving or print, its source and date should be given. The mounting, labelling, and collecting, and even the purchasing, should be done, as far as possible, by the pupils, the teacher being prime director and adviser. Of maps, the best available collection for most of our schools is that of Labberton; and his last edition is accompanied by a full text, which makes it a good work of reference as well. But this collection should be duplicated and supplemented by maps of the pupils' own making. These may be quickly and effectually made by using Heath's *Outline Maps of Ancient History, Europe, Central and Western Europe, British Isles, England, France, Germany, Italy, Greece, etc.*,[1] and filling in the historical part with colored pencils, ink, or, when pupils are so inclined, they may be more elaborately finished with water-colors. A sheet of such little maps of France, for instance, showing her territorial divisions and boundaries at different dates, would make an excellent graphical presentation of much of her history.

Closely allied to maps are graphical representations of time, which are a powerful aid in remembering the relation and sequence of dates. There are several publications which present history in this way; Lyman's *Historical Chart* (Philadelphia) being one of the best. But far better than any prepared work of this kind are century-maps, as they may be called, done by the pupils themselves. At the very beginning of his study, the student should provide himself with as many sheets of good stout paper as there are centuries in his proposed course.[2] The ordinary sermon size will be convenient, and some arrangement should be made by which, as the study progresses, these sheets may be fastened together like a long folding map, so as to give the eye a continuous representation of

---

[1] For the graphic representation, by the pupil of geography, geology, history, meteorology, economics, and statistics of all kinds. Two cents each; per hundred, $1.50. Map of Ancient History, three cents each; per hundred, $2.50.

[2] The ordinary stout manilla paper, sold at a few cents a yard, is heartily recommended for these mounts.

the time considered. Each of these sheets should be boldly and strikingly headed by its own century, each should bear in separate colors the countries considered, and each should have its two or three leading events, names, or movements heavily and clearly printed out. The principle underlying such representations is, that visible place-relations are of great value to the average mind in fixing and remembering the more abstract relations of time. But within the boundaries of this principle, the pupil should be left very free to fill out his century-map in the style, proportion, and detail which best suits him, since the more closely the work is done in accordance with individual taste and aptitudes, the more strongly will it grow into the memory as a permanent acquisition.

Of books it is more difficult to form a collection; and yet some accessible collection is necessary, and the more of it that can be placed in the class-room itself, the better. The teacher needs at least four different kinds of books, each kind having its own power and worth. He needs a full and accurate collection of dates, facts, and names, well indexed; the best single work of this sort is perhaps Tillinghast's *Ploetz' Epitome of Universal History*. He needs a good modern narrative, which shall embody the results of the best scholarship, and serve as a guide to proportion and completeness; such an aid is to be found in Freeman's *General Course*. If he has access to a library, or the means to form one, he wants to know what are the best books on any part of his subject, and the value and contents of others; such an aid he will find in Adams' *Manual of Historical Literature*. A shorter and very useful bibliography of the subject has been made by Prof. W. F. Allen of Wisconsin University, and is published in Hall's *Methods of Teaching and Studying History*.[1] These aids being obtained, the teacher is ready to buy and use advantageously books of a fourth class, — books which bring him as near as possible to the deeds, the

---

[1] This bibliography adds also an excellent short list of historical novels, poems, and plays. The publishers are D. C. Heath & Co., Boston.

lives, the thoughts and feelings, of historic eras and peoples. Of these books, Plutarch's Lives deserves the first place in the list. But, whether much or little can be done to obtain such expressions of the past, teacher and pupils can at least co-operate to preserve for the school some collection illustrative of the present time. If the means are not available for keeping the complete file of a first-class paper, and even if they are, teacher and pupils should collect newspaper clippings, pamphlets, notices, and other ephemeral publications which contain significant speeches, letters, arguments, or striking accounts of contemporary events by the actors or witnesses. Such collections grow rapidly in value. Such materials dating from the Civil War or from the preceding slavery contest are already difficult to obtain, though full of historic interest and instruction; and our own time has as surely its desirable, though ephemeral, records. Such materials as these might be kept in a series of annual scrap-books, or in large manilla envelopes, enclosed in covers, classified according to years or half-years. A good plan is to keep pictures, maps, and scraps on mounts of the same size, or that may be folded to the same size, and to arrange them, without regard to subject, in alphabetical order, in stiff, clearly-labelled covers. Others may prefer to arrange them by topics; but such collections are rather like a dictionary or cyclopedia than a narration, and the alphabetical plan requires fewest cross-references. But teachers need never hesitate at the labor of making rearrangements, whenever it seems desirable; since such work is of great value to pupils, as well as very agreeable to them, *provided you do not ask them to do their own work over.*

Such a material equipment as that above indicated is the very least that any teacher of general history should demand of himself and his patrons. Where means and opportunities are more generous, the teacher should extend his aids as rapidly as possible, having due regard to the properties of his subject and the ability and available time of his students.

He will find that the purchases which will pay best in interest and enthusiasm are books of the fourth class named above, — books which may be described as those of the earliest or contemporary sources (*List D*).

In making the following list, books of the first three classes are named, as well as those of the fourth, since many schools are so situated as to have access to no large library. In such cases, enough of the first three classes must be purchased to render the sources intelligible; where larger purchases of such works are within the means of the school, the buyer should carefully consult Adams' Manual.

A. BOOKS COVERING THE WHOLE FIELD OF GENERAL HISTORY.

Adams, Charles K. Manual of Historical Literature. New York, 1882. $2.50. A descriptive and critical bibliography of the whole subject, including an especially fine portion on United States history.

Bagehot, Walter. Physics and Politics, or thoughts on the application of the principles of natural selection and inheritance to political society. London and New York, 1873. $1.50.

"I only profess to explain what seem to me the political prerequisites of progress, and especially of early progress. . . . Here physical causes do not create the moral, but moral create the physical."

Freeman, Edward A. General Sketch of History. London and New York, 1880. $1.00. A complete, compact narrative, accurate, well-proportioned, philosophical.

Haydn, J. Dictionary of Dates. New York, 1885. Eighteenth edition, revised to date. $5.00. A full and standard work of reference, in which events and names are arranged alphabetically, with full dates and summary descriptions.

Labberton, Robert H. New Historical Atlas and General History. New York, 1886. $2.40. 198 colored maps and 30 genealogical charts. The maps are admirable for the uses of the class-room, or for any student who is making his first acquaintance with the study of General History since they are diagrammatic and free from detail.

Ploetz, Carl. Epitome of Ancient, Mediæval, and Modern History. Translated, with extensive additions, by William H. Tillinghast. Boston and New York, 1884. $3.00. This work can hardly be overestimated as a handbook of general reference; it is very fully indexed, and the matter is arranged in periods and by countries. It is especially valuable in modern history for the full summaries that are given of treaties.

Sheldon, M. D. Studies in General History. Boston, 1885. $1.60. Contains many illustrative extracts from original sources.

Thomas. Universal Pronouncing Dictionary of Biography and Mythology. Titled on back as Lippincott's pronouncing biographical dictionary. Philadelphia, 1886. One volume, $12.00; two volumes, $15.00. The standard dictionary of this sort in English.

[Since new editions are constantly appearing of some of the above works, care should be taken in purchasing, to insist always on the latest in the market.]

B. BOOKS COVERING THE WHOLE FIELD OF ANCIENT HISTORY, OR OF GREEK AND ROMAN HISTORY.

Fustel de Coulanges. The Ancient City. A Study on the Religion, Laws, and Institutions of Greece and Rome. Edited in translation from the latest French edition, by Willard Small. Boston, 1874. $2.00. This book is perhaps the best single volume that can be read in order to gain an insight into the underlying principles, tendencies, and character of antiquity. The author is brilliant, philosophical, and scholarly.

Reber, Franz von. History of Ancient Art, with 310 illustrations. Published in translation from the German. New York, 1882. $2.50. This work covers the whole field for Egypt, Assyria, Persia, Greece, and Rome; and its excellent and numerous pictures make it invaluable.

Sheldon, M. D. Studies in Greek and Roman History. Boston, 1886. $1.00. Simply the first half of the "Studies in General History."

Smith, Philip. A History of the World, from the Earliest Records to the Present Time. Only Ancient History finished, in three volumes. London and New York, 1866. $6.00. An excellent narrative history of the whole period of ancient history, including that of Egypt, Assyria, Babylonia, Judæa, Persia, Greece, and Rome. Its style is easy, and embellished with many extracts from original sources. Adams recommends it as the product of "a careful and judicious observer."

Smith, William. Dictionary of Greek and Roman Antiquities. New York, 1843. $6.00. The standard work on this subject, and rendered still more valuable by many cuts from ancient coins, reliefs, etc.

C. BOOKS COVERING THE WHOLE FIELD OF MODERN, MEDIÆVAL, OR OF MODERN AND MEDIÆVAL HISTORY.

There is no single work in English which covers the modern and mediæval periods so admirably as Philip Smith's *History of the World* covers the field of antiquity; although, in French, Victor Duruy's manuals of Mediæval and Modern History[1] cover the field admirably, being scholarly, vivid, and rich in illustration. Of books accessible in English, the following are recommended: —

Bryce, James. The Holy Roman Empire. New York, 1877. $1.75. A sketch of the first importance for understanding the organic connections of ancient and modern history, of Church and State, of the Papacy and the Empire, from the beginning of our era to the present time.

Dyer, Thomas Henry. The History of Modern Europe from the Fall of Constantinople in 1453 to the close of the Crimean War in 1857. Five volumes. London, 1861. $22.50. A standard, very full, and accurate work of reference, in narrative form.

Gibbon, Edward. The History of the Decline and Fall of the Roman Empire. The best edition is that of Dr. Smith. London. Eight volumes. New York, 1880. Six volumes. $12.00. This classical work is still a rich repertory of material for all the centuries, from the age of Trajan and the Antonines, to the taking of Constantinople

---

[1] "Histoire du Moyen Age" and "Histoire des Temps Modernes"; each of these is published in a single moderate 12mo volume.

by the Turks in 1453. The notes of this edition, by Milman and Guizot, add greatly to its value. Although Gibbon was the first to give a just estimate of the life and work of Mohammed, still this portion of his work, perhaps, most requires the supplement of modern scholarship. The best single book to furnish this is, in my judgment, R. Bosworth Smith's *Mohammed and Mohammedanism.* New York, $1.50.

Guizot, François. History of Civilization in Europe. Paris, 1831. Translations published in New York and London. Two volumes. $4.00. " Perhaps no other historical book is capable of stirring more earnest and fruitful thought in a thoughtful student." — ADAMS.

Lacroix, Paul. The Arts in the Middle Ages and at the Period of the Renaissance.

Manners, Customs, and Dress during the Middle Ages.

Military and Religious Life in the Middle Ages and at the Period of the Renaissance.

The Eighteenth Century; its Institutions, Customs, and Costumes.

Science and Literature in the Middle Ages and at the Period of the Renaissance.

Five volumes; large octavo. London, 1880. Edited in translation from the French. Lacroix was long curator of the Library of the Arsenal in Paris; and these books derive their great value from their wealth of fac-simile illustration, drawn from contemporary manuscripts, coins, carvings, and their numerous cuts of buildings, monuments, furniture, armor, etc. They were originally published at $12.00 a volume, and that is still their price in first-class binding, and with all their fac-similes; but copies can be obtained bound in cloth, and lacking the colored reproductions, for much less, and almost as valuable for school purposes. The volumes are sold separately. The most useful ones for general use are " The Arts" and " Military and Religious Life." Second-hand copies can occasionally be obtained.

Morris, Edward A. [editor]. Epochs of History. London. A series of 16mo vols., republished in New York from time to time by the Scribners, and sold separately at $1.00 a volume. Especially valuable for the general student are the numbers on *The Crusades, The Thirty Years' War, The Puritan Revolution, The Beginning of the Middle Ages, The French Revolution,* and *The Era of the Protestant Revolution.*

Sheppard, John G. The Fall of Rome and the Rise of the New Nationalities. A series of lectures on the connection between ancient and modern history. London and New York, 1861. $2.50. "Large dependence on original authorities." — ADAMS. Gives an excellent foundation for an understanding of the Middle Age.

White, Rev. James. The Eighteen Christian Centuries. London and New York. Second edition, 1862. $2.00. A short, vivid review of the leading events and characters from the time of Christ to the present day.

D. TRANSLATIONS, REPRINTS, AND ABRIDGMENTS OF CONTEMPORARY OR ORIGINAL SOURCES.

[When books are described as belonging to the *Bohn Libraries*, it is understood that they are published in London and New York, and that they cost from $1.40 to $2.00 per volume. The American publishers are Scribner and Welford.]

Ammianus Marcellinus, The Roman History of, during the Reigns of . . . Constantius, Julian, Jovianus, Valentinian, and Valens. Edited in translation as one volume; Bohn's Libraries. Adams describes it as "accurate, faithful, impartial." It is, moreover, vivid.

Arrian. The Anabasis of Alexander; or, the History of the Wars and Conquests of Alexander the Great. Translated from the Greek by E. J. Chinnock. London, 1884. $3.00. Arrian flourished in the first part of the second century of our era; but his book is one of the most "accurate and authentic" of historical works.

Bede. Ecclesiastical History of Great Britain and the Anglo-Saxon Chronicles. Edited by Giles, in Bohn's Libraries. $2.00. Bede covers the period from Cæsar's invasion of Britain to A.D. 664. The "Anglo-Saxon Chronicle" extends from the year 1 to 1154 of our era. That portion of the latter which relates to Alfred the Great, it is believed to be practically the work of his own hand.

Birch, S. Records of the Past; being English Translations of the Assyrian and Egyptian Monuments. Eleven volumes; second edition. London, 1875–1878. $18.00.

Charles, Mrs. E. R. Chronicles of the Schönberg-Cotta Family. New York, 1864. $1.00. This work is so largely a compilation and translation from original and contemporary sources that it forms a valuable addition to any library on the period of the Reformation.

Chronicles of the Crusades. Bohn's Libraries. $2.00. Contains the chronicles of Richard of Devizes and Geoffrey of Vinsauft concerning the crusade of Richard I. of England, Joinville's Memoirs of Louis IX., and extracts from a Saracenic account of the latter King's Crusade.

Chronicles, Six English. Bohn's Libraries. $2.00. Contains the Chronicles of Ethelwerd, Asser's Life of Alfred, Geoffrey of Monmouth, Gildas, Nennius, and Richard of Cirencester. One of the least valuable of the Bohn series for our purposes.

Chronicles of Europe, Early. A series of books put forth by the Society for promoting Christian Knowledge, and containing at present the following three volumes: *Italy*, by Ugo Balzani; *England*, by James Gairdner; and *France*, by Gustave Masson. New York and London, 1883. $1.20 a volume. As an exposition of original sources, the volume on Italy is distinctly the most valuable, containing extracts from Cassiodorus, Gregory the Great, the Chronicle of St. Benedict, the Venetian Chronicle of John the Deacon, the Letters of Gregory VII., and the Chronicles of the Maritime Republics. Aside from the fact that the extracts are more abundant in this volume, the work has also more value from the point of view demanded by general history. The works on England and France are rather of the nature of full descriptive bibliographies, containing also short biographies of the chroniclers. That on France is especially of this nature.

Commines, Philip of. Memoirs. London and New York. Two volumes in Bohn's Libraries. $2.80 each. These memoirs contain the history of Louis XI., Charles VIII., and Charles the Bold, Duke of Burgundy; one of the best of all the chronicles.

Demosthenes, Orations of. Bohn's Libraries. Five volumes. $7.00. The best original we have as showing the situation of affairs and the state of feeling just before the fall of Greece.

Eginhard's Life of Charlemagne. Edited in translation in Harper's Half-hour Series. Twenty cents. Eginhard was the friend and secretary of Charlemagne, and this work is the prime authority for the life of the Great Charles.

Froissart, Sir John. Chronicles of England, France, Spain and Adjoining Countries, from the Latter Part of the Reign of Edward II. to the Coronation of Henry IV. Edited in translation by Thomas Johnes, Esq. Two volumes. London, 1839. $12.00.

For many schools, the *Boy's Froissart* edited by Sidney Lanier, and published in one volume by the Scribners for $3.00, is a very desirable introduction to the expensive original.

Homer. Iliad. Prose translation by Lang, Leaf, and Myers. London, 1883. $1.50.

Odyssey. Prose translation by Butcher and Lang. London, 1879. $1.50. These renderings are especially valuable for historical purposes, being at the same time exact and beautiful. Bryant's translation of Homer is also heartily recommended, especially for younger pupils.

Herodotus. A New English Version. Edited with notes and essays . . . by Canon Rawlinson, Sir H. Rawlinson, and Sir J. G. Wilkinson. With maps and woodcuts. Four volumes. London and New York, 1859. $10.00. " By far the most valuable version." — ADAMS. Also in Bohn's Libraries. One volume. $2.00. Herodotus is our great original for all the history of Greece to the end of the Persian wars. For these wars his account is contemporary and of the first importance. He tells us much also of Egypt and the East.

Livy, Titus. The History of Rome. Edited in translation from the Latin by George Baker. Two volumes. New York, 1861. $7.50. Also in four volumes in Bohn's Libraries. $8.00. Of the one hundred and forty-two original books of Livy, only thirty-five remain. These comprise an interrupted history of Rome from its foundation to 166 B.C. The most valuable part is that which deals with the Punic wars.

Luther, Martin. Table-talk. Translated by Hazlitt. Bohn's Libraries. $1.40. A selection is made in one of the little volumes of Cassell's National Library. Price ten or twenty-five cents, according to binding. Most valuable to give the spirit, thought and feeling of Luther.

Mazade, Charles de. Count Cavour. New York. $3.00.

This work is so rich in Cavour's own words that it becomes a fine contemporary source for the diplomatic and political history of the first half of our century.

Mazzini, Joseph. Life and Writings. London, 1864–1870. An abridgment of this, with an introduction by William Lloyd Garrison, under the title of *Joseph Mazzini: his Life, Writings, and*

Political Principles (New York, 1872. $1.75), will, perhaps, be as useful for the majority of school libraries. This life, covering the long and important period from 1809 to 1872, and being the autobiography of a man who was at the very heart of the movements for national independence and constitutional government, is, perhaps, the best single primary source which can be named for this aspect of our nineteenth-century history.

Mead, Edwin D. [editor]. Old South Leaflets. These leaflets are invaluable for the teacher of United States History. Each one contains an important document or extract illustrative of our history, such as pages from De Tocqueville's *Democracy in America*, Cotton Mather's *Magnalia*, the *Federalist*, etc. Sold at five cents apiece. $3.00 per hundred. They can be obtained of D. C. Heath & Co., Boston.

Ordericus Vitalis. Ecclesiastical History of England and Normandy. Four volumes. Bohn's Antiquarian Library. This history begins at the year 1 of our era and continues to 1141. From 1075, Ordericus is a contemporary of the history he relates, and tells the story of this important formative period both for England and Normandy. He is a prime authority for these years, and particularly valuable as giving a view of manners and of the political and religious state of contemporary society.

Pellico, Silvio. My Ten Years' Imprisonment. London and New York, 1866. Cassell's National Library. Ten or twenty-five cents, according to binding. This little book throws a vivid light on despotism, seen from the point of view of an imprisoned Italian patriot.

Pepys, Samuel. Diary. Four volumes. In Bohn's Libraries. $8.00. For most schools, however, the three little volumes of extracts from the "Diary" for 1660-1661, for 1662-1663, and for 1663-1664, in Cassell's National Library (each volume ten or twenty-five cents, according to binding) will give quite enough of this old gossip, who has preserved for us so exact a picture of the Restoration Court.

Plutarch. The translation from the Greek, known as Dryden's, edited by Arthur Hugh Clough, is on the whole the best. Five volumes. Boston, 1875. $3.00. Also in one large octavo volume. Also in Bohn's Libraries. Four volumes. Also in a cheap edition published by Alden of New York. A number of the "Lives" can be bought in Cassell's National Library. Contains forty-six lives of famous

Greeks and Romans; a work of capital importance in every school library.

Powell, F. York [editor]. English History from Contemporary Writers. London and New York, 1887, etc. This is the name under which Mr. Powell is editing a series of little volumes, each one devoted to a "well-defined portion of English History," and composed of "extracts from the chronicles, state papers, memoirs, and letters of the period considered, the whole arranged in chronological order, and accompanied with summaries for reference." Of this most admirable series four volumes have already appeared, namely, *Edward III. and his Wars*, *The Misrule of Henry III.*, *Strongbow's Conquest of Ireland*, and *Simon de Montfort and his Cause*. These books are rendered still more valuable by the illustrations, which are reproductions from contemporary coins, manuscripts, reliefs, carvings. The American edition costs 60 cents a volume, the English, a shilling (25 cents).

Rémusat, Madame de. Memoirs, 1802, 1808. Published in translation in one volume. $2.00. New York, 1888. Madame de Rémusat was one of Josephine's maids of honor, and her book gives an inside view of Napoleon's character as seen at home. The memoirs as they stand were written from memory, the first copy having been destroyed.

Saint-Simon, the Duke of. Memoirs of the Reign of Louis XIV. and the Regency. Translated from the French, in an abridged edition of three octavo volumes, by Bayle St. John. London, 1876. Three volumes. $6.00. This book, says Adams, was probably "the severest blow the Bourbons ever received."

Schaff, Philip. The Creeds of Christendom; with a history and critical notes. Four volumes. New York, 1877, etc. $16.00. This work contains the formal creeds and official statements of doctrine, from the Apostles' Creed to the present time.

Scoones, W. Baptiste. Four Centuries of English Letters: selections from the correspondence of 150 writers, from the period of the "Paston Letters" (fifteenth century) to the present day. London, 1883. $2.40. The selection is made on the basis of style or contents. Their interest is rather social than political.

Story of the Burnt Njal. Edited by G. W. Dasent. Two volumes. London. $7.50. This is an admirable version of an old Icelandic

Saga, in which, more closely, perhaps, than in any other single work, one can see reflected the manners, temper, institutions, and character of our Teutonic ancestors. Unfortunately, it is now very rare, and brings a high price.[1]

Suetonius. Lives of the Twelve Cæsars [Julius Cæsar to Domitian, inclusive]. One volume. In Bohn's Classical Library. $2.00. Although Suetonius is a standard authority for this subject, he is a much less desirable original to possess than Tacitus or Plutarch, since the last-named writers join to historic faithfulness the highest excellences of style.

Tacitus, C. Cornelius, The Works of. Edited in translation. Two volumes in Bohn's Library. $4.00. Contents: Annals and History of the Empire during the first century A.D. to the accession of Vespasian, including account of the Jews; a treatise on the situation, manners, and inhabitants of Germany; the life of Agricola; a dialogue on Oratory. One of the first originals to be obtained.

Thucydides. The History of the Peloponnesian War. Edited in translation by B. Jowett. Two volumes. London and New York, 1881. Vol. I., Translation; Vol. II., Notes, Essays, and Dissertations. $8.00. A brilliant translation of a great original. Less expensive but still good is the version to be obtained in Bohn's Classical Library. Two volumes. $2.80.

---

[1] Lacking this, one might still obtain Dasent's "Popular Tales from the Norse." This book is also rare; but one can easily get Anderson's "Viking Tales of the North," [Chicago, $2.00], or Mabie's "Norse Stories retold from the Edda" [New York, $1.00].

QUESTIONS IN ROMAN HISTORY.

Designed to cover both Sheldon's and Swinton's General Histories.

In answering these questions, the text-book used should be named, as this fact will make a difference in the character and proportion of the answers.

1. Describe the physical geography of Italy, and state its advantages for the development of Roman power. Name the races inhabiting it at the earliest period of its history, and locate each geographically.

2. What was the earliest form of government at Rome? Who were the plebeians? the patricians? Describe the political and social condition of each in the earliest period of Roman history. What was the Comitia Curiata (Curiate Assembly)? The Comitia Centuriata (Centuriate Assembly)?

3. Into what periods may you divide the history of the Roman Republic? Give the bounding dates of each period.

4. What is the story of Cincinnatus? What character did Cincinnatus display?

5. What changes were made in favor of the plebeians from 510 to 264 B.C.? How were these changes brought about? Define or describe each of the following terms: consul, dictator, tribune of the plebs, veto, assembly of the tribes, twelve tables.

6. Tell what you know of the Gallic invasion of Rome.

7. Describe the Roman territory at each of the following dates, — 510 B.C., 264 B.C., 146 B.C., 27 B.C. Characterize and name its government at each of these dates.

8. How did Rome secure and consolidate her conquests? What relations existed between Rome and the Italians before the so-called "Social War"? What duties and privileges distinguished the Roman citizen before this time?

9. What was the origin of the first Punic war? What was its result to Rome? to Carthage?

10. How did the second Punic war come about? In what did the greatness of Hannibal consist? On what occasions did he display this greatness? What was the outcome of the second Punic war?

11. What was the cause and what the result of the third Punic war?

12. What other conquests were made by Rome during the time of the Punic wars?

13. Describe a Roman province as it existed in the last age of the Republic.

14. Contrast the Roman personal character of the fourth with that of the first century B.C. To what do you attribute the change? Contrast the same periods in regard to the Roman political character. Describe the elder Cato (Cato the Censor).

15. What do you understand by an "agrarian law"? Explain the relation between slavery and the small Italian farmers in the latter days of the Republic. What became of the small farmers?

16. Who were the Gracchi and for what did they contend? What parties arose from their contentions, and with what leaders? Which of these two parties did Cæsar represent?

17. What were the conquests of Rome after 146 B.C.? What generals led her in these conquests, and in what war or wars was each famous?

18. Who were involved in the "Social War"? What was its cause, and what its result? What event do you associate with the name of Catiline? What troubles arose from the slaves of Rome?

19. What do you understand by the "Triumvirates"? What was the aim and what the end of each? What decisive battle finally ended each? Describe the relation of Cæsar to Gaul.

20. Describe the crossing of the Rubicon. Under what title and with what powers was Cæsar ruling Rome just before his death? Why and by whom was he slain? Describe the work of Cæsar for Rome. In what did his greatness consist? Compare him with Pericles.

21. Describe the boundaries of the Roman Empire under Augustus Cæsar. Under what forms did he rule? Illustrate.

22. What were the corn-bounties at Rome, and what was their result? The gladiatorial games? What was the Coliseum?

23. What modern countries have been formed from the Roman Empire?

24. What civilizations were included in that empire? Classify the provinces according to their civilizations.

25. What was the greatest period of Roman art and literature? Name four Romans distinguished in these directions.

26. Name four distinguished or remarkable emperors after Augustus, stating in what century, and for what each was famous.

27. What was the Pretorian guard? Describe Roman citizenship as it existed under the early empire. What great change was wrought in regard to it, and by whom, after the days of the Antonines?

28. What great constitutional change was made in the latter part of the third century, and by whom?

29. Name two things for which Constantine is noted.

30. What was the effect of Rome on the provinces? Prove it. Who were the barbarians? What effect had they in Rome?

31. Compare the western and eastern empires of Rome in regard to civilization, language, government, population.

32. Give the striking points in regard to the growth of Christianity within the empire. Why did Rome regard Christianity as dangerous? State the points of opposition and contrast between the Christians and the Pagan empire. What was the relation between Christianity and literature in the last two centuries of the empire?

33. What unity existed in the later Roman empire? What sources of decay and corruption? Illustrate.

34. Contrast the Roman and the Teuton as they were at 400 A.D. What had been the relations of Roman and Teuton before 476 A.D.? Name three of the barbarian leaders, and tell something of each.

35. Describe the so-called "Fall of Rome." To what do you attribute that event?

QUESTIONS IN GREEK HISTORY.

Designed to cover both Sheldon's and Swinton's General Histories.

In answering these questions, the pupil should state which of the two text-books has been used, since the character and proportion of the answers may vary according to this fact.

1. Describe the physical geography of Hellas. Contrast it with that of Egypt and Assyria. What political results followed from its peculiarities? What industrial results? What were its advantages for an early civilization? What ranges of territory were occupied by the Greeks? Name four cities in which Greek power and civilization centred.

2. What great contrast between the history of Egypt or Assyria and that of Greece? Which history is the more valuable to us, and why?

QUESTIONS IN GREEK HISTORY.

3. Write a short description of the Trojan war, giving parties engaged, cause, result, and place. What is the subject and who the author of the Iliad? Of the Odyssey?

4. Describe the Homeric Age in regard to government, the family, religion, ideals of manhood.

5. What were the foreign influences felt by early Greece? In what ways did Greece show something new to the world?

6. Give the periods of Greek history, with their bounding dates. What is meant by an Olympiad?

7. What relation between the Dorian migration and the Greek cities in Asia Minor?

8. What were the two leading states of Greece? Describe each in race, location, character, fame and influence. What great change in their government occurs between the Homeric Age and 500 B.C.?

9. Name three bonds of union felt by all Hellenes. What remark have you to make in regard to the comparative strength of the principles of unity and of localization among them? Illustrate.

10. Who was Lycurgus? Describe the political constitution of Sparta, according to the Lycurgan laws. What was the system of education imposed by them? Describe the results of the Spartan system to the state, the family, the individual.

11. Describe the constitution of Athens before the time of Solon. What great changes were introduced by him?

12. In what sense was Pisistratus a tyrant? How did he gain and how exercise his power?

13. What were the reforms of Clisthenes? After these reforms, what name should be applied to the political constitution of Athens?

14. What was the cause of the Persian wars? Compare the Greek and Persian dominions at 500 B.C. Compare their unity, government, and civilization.

15. Note the chief events from 492–479 B.C. Of these events, which were most decisive or noteworthy? Name and charac-

terize the Greek leaders in these wars. Tell the story of Thermopylæ. What relation between Thermopylæ and Lycurgus?

16. What were the results of the Persian wars to Athens? to Sparta? to Hellas in general?

17. What distinguished the age of Pericles? Name four special directions of Greek greatness during this age.

18. What was the cause of the Peloponnesian war, and what its immediate occasion? What parties were involved in it, and how was each characterized? What were its results to Athens? to Sparta? to Hellas in general?

19. What was the last Greek city to rise to Hellenic power, and who was her most famous leader?

20. Under what leader and by what methods did Macedon obtain Greek supremacy? Who was Philip's chief opponent in Greece, and by what method did this opponent work against him? What position did he desire to acquire for Macedon in relation to the Greek states? Of what importance is the date 338 B.C.?

21. Name the principal points in the route of Alexander's conquests. What countries belonged to his empire? What empire did he obtain possession of? In the name of what people were his conquests made? What was done with his empire at his death? What important and permanent states sprang from it? What were the results of the Alexandrian conquests to civilization? what civilizations did these conquests bring together?

22. What were the Greek leagues? What modern governments do they somewhat resemble?

23. What seems to you to be the general cause of the inability of Greece to stand against Macedon, and later against Rome? What the peculiar excellence of the Greek state? What the peculiar excellence of the Greek character?

DETAILED DIRECTIONS

FOR

MANAGING A LESSON IN SHELDON'S STUDIES IN GENERAL HISTORY.

(Study on page 15.)

1. PREPARATION.

PEOPLE often feel that the study of history is a mass of *reading*. But here, as elsewhere, the first work must be the *study* of a few typical realities. To put some of these typical realities into the hands of every student is the object of the *Studies*; and unless the pupils have extra time or ability, my own judgment is, that at first, their time and attention should be very thoroughly confined to the *Studies*. I think I may say with safety, that there is not a question in the book which may not be answered from the materials furnished in the way of fact or extract, *plus the pupil's intelligent labor and thought*. Extra reading should follow when the pupil has the power and the time to assimilate it, *and not before;* in the latter case it degenerates into mere stuffing. The very essence of the method here attempted is that it is study, study of reality; one live bird is better than a case full of stuffed ones. If your pupil approaches the study of anatomy for the first time, you don't confuse him by presenting too many creatures at once, you stick pretty closely to the cat, the frog, the chicken, — in short, to your accessible types. So, in the *Studies*, I have tried to collect typical materials on which the first rude general work should be done. Afterwards comes the time for the general reading which will strengthen, extend, and adorn knowledge. This, then, decides the nature of the preparation: it must be study, not reading; it must consist, for the pupil, in working out the answers to the problems set on a given text as independently as if he were doing a problem in algebra or a translation in Cæsar. For instance, suppose it is the second question on page 15 : *Make a list of all the arts and sciences that are indicated by the pictures. (See note also.)* The pupil will turn to the picture of the colossal Rameses on page 11 and begin to ask himself: What arts or sciences must one have known to do this ? Probably *sculpture* will occur to him at once. Then he will see from the note that this Rameses is cut from solid rock, so he will notice *stone-cutting.* Then his mind will run back and ask : What must he have known in order to cut stone, and the answer will come, — he must have had stone-cutting tools, either of metal or of harder stone ; but from the fineness and smoothness of the work on Rameses' face, these tools must have been of metal; and if he used metal tools, he must have known the arts of mining and of metal-working, and so, something of the sciences of *chemistry* and *metallurgy.* Then, turning to the picture of the pyramids, he will work in the same way, looking and thinking of the meaning of what he sees ; the picture of the pyramids, taken in connection with the descriptive note attached, will confirm the list already made and add to it *astronomy, geometry, engineering, quarrying, river-navigation, physics.* So with each question given, he must work its answer out by observation of and reflection upon the given material.

If the teacher is using the *Studies* for the first time, he must prepare his own lesson in the same way as the pupil does; but to facilitate his work, I have in the appropriate place in the manual given him the *clue* to the answers expected, embodying them in the text or in the summaries. He must also have in his mind a clear summary of the points that he wishes to make with his class, and be himself as familiar as possible with the given texts or facts of the *Studies*. But if the teacher is doing this work for the second or third time, his time will be best spent in reading some good authority on the matter in hand, as, in the lesson referred to above, — Wilkinson's *Ancient Egyptians.*

If this, too, has been done, he may come to the truly enlivening part of his preparation, the gathering of new illustrative material for himself and his class out of accessible originals, such as *The Records of the Past*, or some of the reports on Egyptian exploration made in the *Century* articles.

In fact, the teacher should press on to work of this nature as rapidly as possible, since, from that time on, he and his pupils will feel the true breath of life in all their studies. I do not believe any teacher can attain the spiritual quality of enthusiasm, who is not a student of the realities of his subject; so long as he is shut up to what the books say, his work will be positive, indeed, but positive because cut and dried; let him not only be a student, but let the pupils see and feel him to be such; let them share his doubts, his ignorance, his discoveries and pleasures: that is true intellectual life.

2. GENERAL DIRECTIONS FOR THE RECITATION.

The teacher should question rather from his summary than from the set questions of the book; the latter plan tends to make the work dull and stiff. The pupil, besides, has already had the benefit of these book-questions in his private study; in fact, the teacher should use the book in the class only for reference, and be as free from it as he expects his pupils to be; the recitation should give new points of view, the discussion be perfectly free, calling for readiness and wit.

3. PARTICULAR SKETCH OF A PART OF THE CLASS-ROOM WORK ON THE LESSON ON PAGE 15.

Teacher. Alice and Henry may go to the board and write their lists of the arts and sciences known to the Egyptians, while the rest of us talk about the religion. How do we know that they had any religion, anyway, Philip?

Philip. Why, because they prayed.

Teacher. And how do you know that?

Philip. Because we have their prayers; there is the prayer to the sun, and the prayer of Rameses, and the prayer to the Chief God.

Teacher. What other proof that they had a religion?

Anna. We know that they had temples, from the pictures of them, and from the lists of buildings made by the kings.

Laura. They had images of the gods, and sang hymns to them.

Teacher. What proof have you of that?

Laura. Because there is a picture of one of these images, and we have one of the hymns to the Nile.

Teacher. Well, I think we may fairly put down religion as a part of the old Egyptian life. (Writes it on the board in proper place in the summary already begun in a previous lesson. See *page 4, Manual.*) And now, what about the number of the gods, James?

James. They had, at least, several.

Teacher. For instance?

James. They worshipped the Nile, the sun, a god that they call the Lord of Truth, and another that they call Ammon.

Teacher. Do you know how we describe a religion where the people believe in more than one god. (No one answers. The teacher should never wait long for a technical or unknown word, but should give it himself if the class does not at once supply it.) We call it *Polytheistic.* (Writes the word on the board, under Religion.) And what sort of objects are the Nile and the sun, Carlton?

Carlton. Why, I suppose we might call them natural.

Teacher. (Writes on the board *Nature-worship,* after Polytheistic.) What did they see in the Nile to worship? Jenny, what do you say?

Jenny. The Nile gave them life.

Teacher. How so?

Jenny. Why, the Nile made the grass grow in the meadows, and the grass fed the oxen and made them live and grow, and then the oxen fed men and made them live and grow.

Teacher. And what about the Nile?

Jenny. Nobody fed that, so far as they could see.

(Here is a place where it is quite appropriate for the teacher to add something himself to the general fund; he may call attention to the fact that the Nile was the *one* river of Egypt, and a branchless river, coming eternally full of life-giving water from some unknown source. The reasons why the sun would seem divine should then be discussed in the same way; such a talk brings the pupil into historic sympathy with the old Egyptian's point of view, and he comes to feel that, after all, the old fellow was kith and kin of his own, and that he, too, would have been an old Egyptian once upon a time.)

Teacher. Now we have just been saying that the religious belief was polytheistic; now, do you know, that doesn't seem quite true to me; does it to you, Will? Did you see anything to make you think that they had a tendency to believe in one god; that is, to be *monotheists ?*

Will. It says in one place, "prayer to the Chief God."

Teacher. Yes; but is there any proof in the prayer that he is chief? (No one knows.) I think you could easily have seen that; but now look again at this prayer. (All open their books to page 10. There is a moment's silence.) Ah! some of you see already; what do you see, Mary?

Mary. He seems to have made the other gods; for it says, — *at whose command the gods were made.*

John. And he is greater than the Nile; for it says, — *at whose pleasure the Nile overflows her banks.*

Teacher. Good; that wasn't so hard to see, after all. (This is the way in which total failure on the part of the pupils must be met, when the teacher is sure such failure is not due to carelessness. In the latter case, the teacher will simply leave the matter for another trial on the following day; but, at the beginning of the work, before pupils understand very clearly what is expected of them, it is well for the teacher to help them by doing some actual study with them in the classroom. Such help should not be given afterward, except in cases where the teacher sees that the question is really too difficult for the average of the class, in which case it is always best to have recourse to the text on the spot.) So you see that though the Egyptians believed in many gods, — they believed, in fact, in many more than those named here, — yet they also had the thought of one god above all gods; so, we must add *Tendencies to Monotheism* here to Polytheistic Nature-worship. Now, what did they think about the immortality to the soul? Kate, what do you say?

Kate. They believed in it; at least, in the Book of the Dead, the soul is represented as coming before Osiris after death for judgment, and then, if Osiris is contented with it, going on to Elysium.

Teacher. And what about the bodies?

Mary. They embalmed them; put them up to keep.

Teacher. Perhaps some of you know from your general reading why they wanted to keep the bodies; well, Mary again?

Mary. They thought some day that the soul would want the body again.

Will. Why, that is just what we Christians believe about the resurrection of the body; we think the soul and body will last forever, too.

Teacher. Yes, a great many people do think so. (The teacher must not allow himself to be drawn off into any statement of *his own belief* here, although to a certain extent he may allow his pupils to express themselves on these delicate religious matters. Teacher writes *Immortality of the Soul*, on the board, under Religion.)

Teacher. Now, when I asked you for proofs that Egyptians had a religion, you said right away "they prayed to the gods"; now what made them pray to the gods, James?

James. Why, because they wanted things, and they thought that the gods could give them to them.

Teacher. What were some of the things they prayed for?

(Various members of the class answer, "Success in war," "Help in trouble," "Justice," etc.)

Teacher. What do such prayers show that they thought of the gods?

Various members. That they were powerful, kind, just.

(Teacher writes on the board *Believed gods would and could help men.* The teacher may, if he thinks best, also call attention to the fact that this is really the belief in special providence.)

Teacher. When you were naming the gods, there was one whom you did not name.

James. Well, I wanted to ask you about the king; it seemed as if they prayed to him, too, just as if he were a god.

Teacher. You are quite right. The king was like a god to them; just turn to page 14, and see how they address him; read a sentence, Jenny, in which they speak to him as if he were a god.

(Jenny reads, "Hail to thee, Horus, sacred majesty"; others read other sentences showing the same thing. The teacher then asks, "Mary, do you remember from our lesson of yesterday another fact that shows that the religion had a good deal to do with the government?")

Mary. Yes; the king was a priest, and the chief high priest was next to the king.

Other members give other facts, as that the king was always building temples, that the priests held many offices, etc. Teacher writes on the board, *Close union of religion with the state, as shown in importance of temples and priests, and sacredness of king.*

Meanwhile the lists have been placed on the board, and the teacher will proceed in a similar way to collect the points for the intellectual, industrial, political, social, and moral life of the ancient Egyptians, as per summary. In this sort of work, the teacher will notice, *first,* — that the questions follow a summary in his own mind, rather than the order of questions in the book; as has been already said, this gives freshness and order to the work. *Second,* — new terms are given at once, as soon as, but *after,* the thing they name is understood; examples, Polytheism, Nature-worship, Monotheism. *Third, — and greatest of all, constant reference must be made to the text.* It *must be appealed to as proof of the pupils' statements, and be their referee in all cases of dispute. In short, it must be used just as the specimen would be used in botany;* and if the teacher has been able to collect still other material from the sources, it should be used similarly, to prove, test, modify, or broaden opinion.

The above has been written on the supposition that the teacher is as yet in the "little go" of his teaching, and is still confined to his text-books in hand; if, however, he has had time to do further reading, or if, best of all, he has had time to hunt up new pictures and extracts, he will be able to enrich every moment of the hour. In the latter case, however, there is real danger of his getting in the way of the pupil, and he must always remember that he is in the class-room, first of all, to give full play to the pupils. Let *their own work* stand out simple, clear, and strong, rectified by your own greater knowledge and judgment.

What the teacher brings from his own stores should be connected with what the pupils have themselves done. It should be illustrative and cumulative in its effect, and be in plain sight from their elementary point of view. But, keeping this primal principle in view, let him go as far afield with them as he possibly can.

MARY SHELDON BARNES.

www.ingramcontent.com/pod-product-compliance
Lightning Source LLC
Chambersburg PA
CBHW020904230426
43666CB00008B/1312